HEARTLANDS
A MAGAZINE OF MIDWEST LIFE & ART

INTRODUCTION
ON PUBLISHING A MIDWEST MAGAZINE OF WRITING AND LIFE

In the fall of 2005 a group of us editors drove to Bowling Green State University for a national conference on writing and publishing. We come from different parts of the state and meet most frequently near publication dates to set the vision and layout of each issue. So that day we came together with other writer-editors (Let's face it, most of the editors of such non-commercial publications are writers themselves. Who else would work so hard for so little at publishing?). During the panel, we heard and learned from each other about our group intention and methods.

For example, one question was about how Connie Willett Everett manages to read the mountain of short fiction that comes in. I know as a review editor that I have to beat the bushes to find folks who will review "The Best of the Midwest" writing. In her case, the manuscripts search her out in gangs. Turns out, that when Connie has read through about 20 or so, she gets a feel for where the material is going. She begins to shop for pieces that will work together in some loose way, and she takes whole days to do her readings…one right after the other. Nancy Dunham also searches out nonfiction, often working with writers who query her about pieces. Mixing articles and personal essays, and after sharing with the other editors, she discovers what works for each issue. I know she has a hard time saying no to anyone with talent.

Our poetry editors, David Shevin and Lin Ryan-Thompson actually work independently (David lives in Dayton, Lin in Huron (and now near Toledo), so they grant each other a right to make half the selections, and share material at the editors meeting. Becky Dickerson rounds up what photos she can from some of her photography classes at Lorain County Community College, plus scouts out area photographers and deliberates over the photos that have come in. As managing editor of *Heartlands* as well as director of Bottom Dog Press, I've been lucky enough to spot some fine artists and photographers to supply our cover images. The articles on writing and nature and life in our region typically come from within our Firelands Writing Center group of writers. Wilma Daugherty and I keep track of the manuscripts and get them out to the genre editors. Yvonne Stella picks up the slack and helps us image the magazine. The editors and FWC group copyedit the magazine for errors. It's a cooperative effort.

The person I have left out so far, is my co-managing editor Susanna Schwacke, perhaps the hardest worker in the group. She is involved at all stages, but primarily pulls it all together in the layout of the publication. Oh, the editors meet, share and envision each volume, but Susanna manages the material into a coherent design when it comes in. Our writers and artists typically send material to her as Word documents or jpg's, which she then reformats into a PageMaker publication for the printer. She also does the ads and credits pages. I coordinate with her in rounding up all of this material. And somehow, some how, it all comes out as *A Magazine of Midwest Life and Art*.

Of course, we couldn't do any magazine without the generous contribution of material from our writers and artists, as well as financial support from our university, patrons, and the Ohio Arts Council. In the end our shared hope is that we have created something of strength and beauty by our region's writers and artists, and for a wide community of its readers: *The Heartlands*.

-Larry Smith, Managing Editor

EDITORIAL STAFF:

Larry

Susanna

Yvonne

Becky

MANAGING EDITOR...LARRY SMITH
MANUSCRIPT MANAGER... WILMA DAUGHERTY
CO-MANAGING EDITOR............................SUSANNA SHARP-SCHWACKE
LAYOUT/DESIGN....................................SUSANNA SHARP-SCHWACKE
ASSISTANT MANAGER.....................................YVONNE STELLA
PHOTOGRAPHY EDITOR.................................BECKY DICKERSON
NONFICTION EDITOR......................................NANCY DUNHAM
FICTION EDITOR................................CONNIE WILLETT EVERETT
POETRY EDITOR...................DAVID SHEVIN & LIN RYAN-THOMPSON
REVIEW EDITOR... LARRY SMITH
COPY EDITORS..............................STAFF & MEMBERS OF
                                    THE FIRELANDS WRITING CENTER

Nancy

Connie

David

Lin

ALL WORKS REPRODUCED HEREIN HAVE BEEN DONE SO BY PERMISSION OF THE ARTISTS/WRITERS.
COVER ART BY BRUCE SELYEM, 2006©.
ADDITIONAL ART BY SUSANNA SHARP-SCHWACKE©.

PUBLISHED BY:

THE FIRELANDS WRITING CENTER
OF BGSU FIRELANDS

ONE UNIVERSITY DR., HURON, OHIO 44839

WITH SPECIAL THANKS TO THE:

Ohio Arts Council
FOR ITS CONTINUED SUPPORT.

ISBN: 1-933964-02-2

TABLE OF CONTENTS:

NEAR-SIGHTED VISION
KAYE BACHE-SNYDER

On this dark, winter morning, I root in the dresser drawer for my warmest cardigan—an old, hand-knit, Norwegian ski sweater. I'm used to fumbling for my clothes, because I dress before putting on my glasses. Such moments I steal to be free of the heavy lenses saddling my nose.

As I touch the sweater's metal buttons, I also hit something sharp and jerk my hand back. Sucking my right thumb, I worm my left hand under the sweater and slide my palm slowly over a cold surface like fine sandpaper. As if reading Braille, I trace its ridges and valleys. Then I know. The ridges form letters and numbers on a rusty license plate that I buried here a few years back.

G - 18 - B
OHIO 1936
"Dad," I whisper. "I'm sorry. Sorry I never thanked you as I should have."

In this darkness, I see and understand. This auto license came in a shoebox in 1993, mailed to me in Colorado from Toledo by my father George Bache. He also enclosed other mementos. A medal he'd won on a motorcycle tour in the Twenties before he married Mom. Two Kresge's snapshots of my sister and me that he'd once kept in his toolbox at work. A diamond lapel pin honoring his 70 years in the Fort Meigs Masonic Order. A *Toledo Blade* clipping from the Forties, headlined "George Bache bowls perfect 300 games at Gazzolo's alleys." Under these lay the 1936 license. It was, I recall, the oldest in his chronology of G-18-B plates saved from his cars.

I resisted the unspoken message of the shoebox: *Here, Kaye, are things precious to me. I want you to have what I won't need any more.* And, maybe: *I want you to know how sad I am.*

"Why is he sending me this stuff?" I said to my husband, who with his usual wisdom did not answer his wife when ruffled. Half-sick, I put some of the mementos in my jewelry drawer. The tour medal. The Masonic pin. The snapshots of my beauty queen, older sister; and of me, a junior high school, not so beauteous grinner. I scrubbed the gasoline smells from the license plate, but couldn't budge the rust. Then I slid it in the bottom of this, my deepest drawer.

Still sucking my sliced thumb, I taste blood and remember one of my Dad's stories. *Lockjaw. A guy at* our plant stepped on a rusty nail, got lockjaw and died. Be careful when you go barefoot, Kaye. Step on a rusty nail and you might get lockjaw. Gets in your blood and kills ya.

Parents keep talking to you, long after they're gone. It's the young father I visualize talking—a wiry, muscular redhead telling stories that contained warnings or preserved humorous moments in our family history. For example, he used to tell the story of my older sister baking him a flat birthday cake. Since the can said it contained "double-acting baking powder," she halved the amount of that ingredient in the recipe. Maybe stories were one of his ways of showing he cared about us, since we were not a family of hugs, kisses and love-you's. Only when Dad reached his 90s did he end his telephone calls with: *I love you*; then, would repeat, before hanging up, his trademark, *Ga-bye. Ga-bye.*

I always bragged to my friends how my father worked as a die-maker until age 84. It was my way to delay facing that he would get as old and rusty as this license plate. It once identified his 1935 Pontiac; the two-door, black car with sloping trunk that he drove to his work during World War II and until 1950. After the faithful Pontiac came the used, two-door, 1949 Desoto with the G-18-B gleaming in a mouthful of chrome on the grille. In 1951, Dad drove the Desoto on our first and last trip as a family of four to the West Coast. His were modest cars until the 1970s. Then one of my parents' square-dancing friends with failing eyesight sold him a luxurious 1972 Chrysler Imperial, dirt-cheap. Dad's car grew longer and larger, as he was beginning to shrink. Around age 90, he began to sit on a cushion to see out the windshield.

Whenever I saw this license plate, I felt safe. Safe he had come to pick me up and confident of his driving. Safe too, as my parents supported me through college and down into my valleys between jobs. They never finished high school, but made sure their two girls had lessons in art, piano, singing, dancing and, later, college and graduate educations.

My left hand still rests on the license plate, warming it. Ohio allowed drivers to keep the same numbers year after year. I remember how Dad nailed his plates—like trophies—on the garage wall from 1936 on. In that and other habits, he was organized. Like father, like daughter. I struggle to keep my drawers, closets, books, journals, notebooks and writing files organized, as if order is protective armor for our inevitable duel with that rider of the pale horse.

His garage gallery of plates reflected how he valued his automobile. He knew his cars inside and out because he made the dies from which transmissions, gears and motors were cast. He was as meticulous in car maintenance as in carpentry around our home. He'd say: *There's a right way to do things.* He showed me, for example, how to measure and saw wood to construct our dog's house. Now I strive to measure words and construct my sentences "the right way," a slow process.

My father must have nailed the final G-18-B plate up in 1991, when his doctor told him not to drive any more. A year later, he telephoned me to vent his anger, as he did when Mom was away. "Do you know what she did, Kaye? Behind my back, she called a damned tow-truck. Got rid of my Chrysler."

To me it seemed the ultimate blow in their 60 years of marital sparring. Mom hadn't driven for eight years because of a disabling stroke. Now she wanted to free up space so their caretaker could park her car there. To Mom it made sense. To him it must have seemed a symbolic castration. Maybe he sent me the 1936 plate as a memorial of the year when his life was an open road, not constrained by a walker.

Years have passed, and with them, my father and mother. Now I am in that reflective period of life through which Dad must have passed before mailing me the shoebox. Like him, I am looking back over a long, eventful and healthy life, but with regret for my unrealized dreams. For years I've wanted and tried to make it as a writer, maybe even as a painter. But I haven't succeeded.

Now it's time to put my valuables in a shoebox. Money, diamonds and heirlooms may be valuable to others, but are different from what I have invested my life in. I listed the conventional valuables in my will, written several years ago. It was a sobering, but easy task, compared with writing the memorandum to the will. I've put off sending my attorney that list of valuables with directions for their distribution. I have no idea where to have them sent.

My husband and I have no children to receive our gifts. Among younger relatives, there are two nephews, a niece and several cousins, all living in other states. It is awkward to ask what they want and, likely, as awkward for them to reply without appearing either greedy, or politely not interested.

I hear my echo: *Why is she sending me this stuff?*

Then there are the things valuable to me: shelves of journals, books, files of writing and that unpublished novel. I'd guess when my father mailed this rusty license, he'd decided to prevent his real valuables from being towed off and junked. Sometimes I imagine that mechanical arm on one of our Longmont garbage trucks reaching down and scattering my novel into a Colorado wind. My words flutter on wings of white paper down our street, some swept away on the grilles of speeding cars.

Feet cold, half-dressed and shivering in this snowy dawn, I lay Dad's license plate on my desk, put on the Norwegian sweater and find my glasses. Staring out windows glazed with ice, I worry. Will I one day be blind? While I can still see, I'll write my way out of the quandary. What is valuable to me and why? I turn on the light and scribble some notes. Eyes watering, the words blur. Yet my vision of the task is clearer now.

There's a right way to do things. "You did it, Dad. I'll try to do as well in saying my final, Ga-bye. Ga-bye."

Kaye Bache-Snyder with her father, George Bache.

FROM *THE ART OF COUNTRY GRAIN ELEVATORS*:
POEMS BY JON VOLKMER
PHOTOGRAPHS BY BRUCE SELYEM

ARROWHEAD, ALBERTA ©

DUST

Some said it was corn
killed a man first.
Something in the particular

smell of corn.
Like coughing up lungfuls
of Green Giant creamed style.

Wilmer figured beans
was the worst.
You don't get your big clouds

with soy beans
But it was oily, you felt it cling
and itch your throat for days.

Wheat can be funny
smelling almost of bread
And the shit you cough up

kind of looks like dough.
I knew milo was worst of all,
because Old Vaughn said so,

and he had to spit out
the oxygen tube
to say so.

WYOLA, MONTANA ©

BEER

Beer recollects brown linoleum,
a banged-up roll top desk with drawers
full of hammers, wrenches, drill bits.

Afternoon shadows of the elm tree play
across the concrete slab unfurled
like a welcome mat outside the office door.

A pick-up rolls to a stop; the scale levers rock.
The gray-haired farmer saunters in, jokes about
the air conditioner peeing on the floor,

and wonders where a hard-working man
might find a beer. Dad says no such characters
have showed up here, and hands the man a beer.

My father drank. He drank beer every day, and
never got drunk. This is not, as you suspect,
a sentimental lie, balderdash about a hollow leg.

He was abstemious, judicious, rigorous
and undeceived. It took me many years
knocking around this booze-beloved earth

to understand how very rare that is.
He scorned the fancy stuff. Storz Triumph,
brewed in South Omaha, was good enough.

Old Doc Anvil, Big John Burgess,
a couple of Kreifels from Talmadge or Brock,
Squeaky Reeky, the Stuckenholtz boys.

HANDSWORTH, SASKATCHEWAN ©

I conjure them from a time before pull tabs,
from hiss of church key piercing steel cans.
I see them settle in broken rocking chairs,

paint-chipped stools, upended five gallon cans.
The light over the propane tank is mellow; Dad
leans his chair back, letting his feet dangle.

Thirteen is old enough to cooper cars,
to handle rat poison and fumigant. It is not
old enough to have a beer of my own.

Dad gives me a sip of his, sometimes
two or three, until I become a pest
and draw the jests of farmers seated round.

Memory is known for its games, and poets
for their lies. This much is true: he sent those men
home sober, and the song he murmured,

driving home, was the one where Perry Como
measured love by the bushel and the peck
and the hug around the neck.

THE ART OF COUNTRY GRAIN ELEVATORS

In August heat, a stalk of corn can yank
its own root-cluster half out of the ground.
So eager to distill minerals, sunshine,
and moisture into gold, it cannot abide
the patient discipline of photosynthesis.
That's the sense of place I'm talking about here.

The field breeds grain; the grain breeds trucks;
the trucks swarm along a railroad track.
From tin and two-by-fours an elevator grows,
and for a span of seasons flourishes,
then withers to dust and blows away.
That's the sense of time I'm talking about here.

Open the tailgate; watch the grain pour
through a slotted metal grate upon the floor.
A fast conveyer belt with cups like bread pans
rattles it upwards to a turntable suspended
in the sky, a small one-windowed room
that elevator men and poets call the head house.

The geyser makes its apogee, and the flow
of grain can be directed and distributed
into bins that hold the offerings
of sundry harvest times, or shot down
into a boxcar bound for the flour mills
of Minneapolis, or the feedlots of St. Paul.

I am the swain of grain, cornball poet
extraordinaire. I am the dust of Silesian
steamer trunks, I'm a cross from County Claire.
Add a mother's death, the evaporated song
of the father she left, and simmer two-score
summers in Nebraska air. I do the silo's

business, preserving what geography and biology
have conspired with time and climate to hoard
in me. What I store up can be dispatched
for someone somewhere's sustenance,
but not unless, and not until,
it has been
elevated.

TUNIS, MONTANA ©

GOOD THUNDER, MINNESOTA ©

ALL ROADS LEAD TO THE COUNTRY
DAVID MICHAEL WOLACH

This time of night it was empty. She'd spent almost two years there working the checkout. The lot and the building were visible only briefly, and then the train pulled in.

Their car was empty as well. An advertisement for a technical school hung on the wall in front of the first row of seats. "Job Training in No Time *Flat,*" it said, and above this was a black man in cap and gown holding a diploma. She pulled the boy down the aisle and made him sit on her lap.

"You okay?" she said.

The boy put his arms around her. The train lurched from the station, its electric cables thwapping against their connecting wire. Those cables stretched for miles, and when she thought about that she tried to imagine a stretch of miles.

"I love you," she said, kissing his forehead.

Diploma. No steel here. No car factories. What's left. *Information Technology.*

Two weeks ago there was a flood in the basement. One of those flash floods that you see on TV. Dogs and horses floating downstream, old men trapped on the roofs of their houses, that kind of thing. It all happened so fast that when she got down there, the whole place was underwater. Dave arrived from work after she telephoned him.

"Trish," he'd said. "What the hell?"

As if it was her fault. As if somehow she had conspired with the weather.

"Look at this," he'd said. "This is nice. This is fucking nice."

Run-off the color of tea rushed in from the street-level windows. It crashed onto the washing machine and dryer. She remembered that just over the weekend she had been sitting on the green arm-chair next to the bookshelf, taking pleasure in watching cars coming and going from the carport, the feet shuffling past. Now the chair was half submerged.

It was quite amazing. Some old Polaroids floated on the surface as more papers were pouring off the shelving units next to the dryer. Bills maybe, old receipts. Chaos, destruction. The sound it made was oppressive, gong-like. She looked at the water and couldn't see into it. She watched it rise.

Dave rubbed the back of his neck. Then he took his pants and dress shirt off, his shoes and socks. He threw them at her and she collected them, took them to the landing. He was standing in nothing but his boxer shorts and somehow this was helpful.

"Jesus Christ," he'd said.

The force of his knuckles tugged at the elastic waistband of his boxers and she could see where his buttocks turned suddenly from tan to alabaster white. She entertained the thought of him falling in, what that might be like. She almost felt her hands give him a little push. Just a small push. To see if he'd go in. But instead she walked right past him like they do in the movies, right down the steps into the water.

"Hey! Trish! You fucking…"

She didn't hear the last part.

Her head was already underneath the water Her eyes were already open. Who knows why, but she had the distinct feeling that there was something to be found down there. She couldn't see an inch past her face but she couldn't hear him either. There was something horrible, something beautiful about being under that water, not being able to see anything but how dirty it was.

The boy put his head on the woman's shoulder as they looked out the window. Every few seconds a street lamp skimmed by. Later, a neon sign appeared that said "Winkleman's Drug and Grocery," and it seemed to be floating just at that place where a horizon would be. It got smaller and eventually disappeared.

The boy fell asleep, too, eventually.

And as the darkness outside became more permanent, the lights inside the train became less tolerable. I'm sick, they seemed to say. I'm a sickly permanence. That was what they said to the woman every now and then.

At one of the stops a man got on the train. He was older, fifty perhaps, tall with thinning hair, and he held something under his arm. It wasn't until he sat down in an aisle seat across from them that she figured out what it was. It was a music box, one of those antique wooden devices that play old rag time or nursery songs. When he sat down he glanced at her bare feet, their tops blackened. He nodded a hello, but she could tell that this detail disgusted him a little.

She kept staring at this box. The cherry wood was worn down and its hinges were rusty. The thing was probably close to a hundred years old. The man noticed that she was looking at it, and so, after some time, said to the boy, "Is that your mom?"

The boy didn't answer. He just sank further into the woman's body. She returned to the window and saw more darkness. And the man saw that the boy was timid, so he said, "Listen," and opened the lid.

Nothing came from it, not a sound. So the woman figured he was one of those. One of those creeps that ride the train. "It's broken," she said.

The man closed the lid and shrugged.

"It's not broken—just plays softly," he said. "Maybe sometime when everything's quiet I'll play it for you. Then you'll hear," he said. He said this as if they would be spending a great deal of time together. And so he was. He was one of those creeps.

They traveled several miles in relative quiet. She'd begun counting the lights over the distant highway. They were rare items in an otherwise seamless darkness, stars on the edge of a galaxy.

Then she heard the man's voice again. It broke a perfectly good silence. He asked her in this fake-curious way what they were doing, what their story was.

"Where are you going at this time of night?" he'd asked.

And something about his tone made her hear the question. Michigan, Detroit. Dave's job gone in a month. Where'd it go? She was just barely seeing beyond the window some cornfields and the shadowy outline of a silo when she said softly, so as not to wake the boy, "I don't know."

© Stephanie Datco, 2006

© Brittany Parfitt, 2006

NEAR STAUNTON MILL
REBECCA LILLY

*

Scented with field grass
the moon-cast shadows of pines
merge in the dampness

*

The mist barely moves
on the mountain peaks; down here,
light rain hits the stream

*

Cedar and fir scent
at the woods edge; water curves
through the settled limbs

*

Parting mist obscures
the full moon; from a pine grove
repeated owl hoots

*

A shift in the breeze
as clouds float over the woods...
stream-flow darkening

BEE HARVEST
WALTER KNUPFER

The ruts in the river glade weave gold
beads of light, goldenrod and sunflowers,
black-eyed Susans burnished at the field's
edge with the itch of autumn, the beans turned
fool's gold this week, earlier than usual, the corn's
gone under, kernels bound for distant markets.

I walk up a pair of herons streaking for their lives
in the river bottom, gnats swarm in the cold eddies,
piercing my genitals, as I climb the embankment
to the baking sand, where the flies feast on my ankles,
craning my neck for the circling herons in the drifted
sands, their former exile, in oxbows, farm ponds

and puddles cut off in the barren prairie
in the wasting sun, riots of monarch butterflies
and katydids dance with the dizzy bees,
crazy for the sugar that they will not get,
the endless summer of their lives, risking
anything in their staggering lust, sucking

and stinging before succumbing to the frost.
What will awaken in the fallow fields,
the born again, the winners or losers,
or the lovers and the lonely, and who will
remember what was loved and what was lost
in the drift of the last bee into flakes of snow?

A DUMB ACCIDENT
KNUTE SKINNER

I placed myself as desired and she proceeded.
Her hand on my calf was about to take my mind
away from my troubles,
but her touch, you know, was only professional.

"I was going to even it up when I fell," I said.
"I'm sure you were," she said, reaching for tape.
When she leaned over my body to the counter,
her dark hair fell away from her neck,
revealing a faint scar.

"It was a dumb accident," I continued,
"but I've been feeling lousy all day.
Otherwise I could have beaten her easy,
especially as she hasn't much of a backhand."
"Yes, maybe so," she said, turning her head.
Her eyes were a mild brown beneath her contacts,
and I wondered how she would look
if she ever smiled.

"It was mostly the junk Mother gave me for breakfast,"
I said, needing someone to be at fault.
"Here, take this,' she responded, producing a pill,
"and lie quiet until the doctor comes.
He should be here in a minute."

When I finished, she took the paper cup
and dropped it into the trash.
Moving quickly, she covered me to my chin,
then stood up tall and looked down on me with a smile.
It wasn't the smile I wanted to see,
and her words were so low that I could scarcely hear them:
"She had you beat and you know it."

THE HANGOVER
KNUTE SKINNER

"It's the goddamned ginger ale
that gives you the goddamned hangover."
She sat there, elbows on table, head on her hands,
and stared at her untouched toast.
"That's what I always say.
How about you?"

"Me, I don't always say anything," I said
as I pulled our blouses and T-shirts out of the washer.
If the weather holds, I was thinking,
they can dry on the line.

"What time is it anyway?" she said
and looked at her wrist as though
she expected to see the watch
she had lost somewhere.
"You'll be late for work, won't you?"

"It's Sunday," I said, "in case you've forgotten.
It's the day even God stays home."
I opened the door and looked outside,
where the sky was depressingly gray.
"And in case you've also forgotten," I added,
"we do have a clock on the wall."

"Will you close that goddamned door," she said,
rousing enough to hug herself.
"That draft would do in a saint."

"Which you are, I suppose," I replied,
slamming shut the door,
"except for the goddamned ginger ale, of course."

"No, there's also the goddamned brandy," she said,
suddenly looking sorry as well as sick.
She gestured me toward her.
"Thank you for closing the door," she said
as I sat beside her and put a hand on her shoulder.

We sat there a while in silence,
then she pinched my leg.
"I'm no saint, as you damned well know,
and as soon as this shit is over,
I'll damn well show you."

SOLIPSISTIC HILLSIDE
DOUG RAMSPECK

Lao Tzu says we know the world
               before even we step into it.
Know the divine from this side of the
               barrier.
Accomplish in life without one single action.

        So as I watch the evening sun slip behind
               this solipsistic hillside—
orange peel sinking and loosening as nightly specter,
enshrouding gaseous coals dimming as the body's
               flame extinguished—
I imagine being drawn into the secret belly,
down into the deepest hidden measure,
where the massive weight of memory
               unravels,
where the massive specter of radiance
               is formed.
And as I sit here on this porch, I remind
myself I have never scaled that hillside in the evening.
Have never ridden bareback on the sun
               as it descends.
But still Lao Tzu is right:
               being and non-being create each other.

THERE IS ONLY NOW.
STEPHEN KOELSCH

The man in a blue jacket reaches
for the dropped pencil. Leaning far
out to his left, his right foot kicks out
like a dancer, performing an arabesque.
His thinning hair, peppered with silver
and grey, reveals a bit of his story.
Worn shoe leather, exposed by his reaching,
tells those of us careful to notice, the way
the world grinds away those parts of one's
self, where pressure has been applied.
We wonder what he will be forced to write,
and which blank spaces he will fill?
Will he write to fill in what has worn away,
in an attempt to restore or explain his reaching?
The hand holding the recovered pencil moves
slowly, perhaps weighing more than it should.

MIDWEST COUNTRY LIFE
AS OBSERVED BY LORAIN COUNTY COMMUNITY COLLEGE
PHOTOGRAPHY STUDENTS

© Mildred Figueroa, 2006

© Danielle Grodek, 2006

© Linnea Satterfield, 2006

© Stephanie Datco, 2006

© Jason Gosnell, 2006

© Stephanie Datco, 2006

© Mildred Figueroa, 2006

© Stephanie Datco, 2006

© Linnea Satterfield, 2006

VELVEETA IS THE ONLY CHEESE

ANNE PANNING

When my Grandpa Pader asks if I want any "sauce," he means canned peaches or pears. If he asks me to stick around for a "little lunch," he means it's probably about 9 p.m., we've been visiting, and he's going to put out a plate of skinless hot dogs, white bread, and creamed green beans. When he asks me if I'm "all," I say "yes, finished." This is code. He's also been known to proclaim, "Velveeta is the ONLY cheese," and then sit with elbows on the table while I try to gag down an inch-thick, quivering slab. He speaks loudly, almost shouting. He weighs in at 280 pounds, and has told me he's pushing for 300. "That's right, kid. You just watch me."

On a visit back to his farm in Green Isle, Minnesota, one summer, I caught him in his basement on the treadmill, wearing his usual dark blue overalls and black socks, drinking a Milwaukee's Best. He huffed and puffed, slurped and guzzled. The belt under his feet ground with friction, and the little speedometer flickered at under five mph. The TV was on full blast: a heavy console sunk into moist, marbled carpet. "This is the way I do it, kid. Doctor told me to exercise. If I'm going to exercise, I need beer. Get yourself one. But remember to close the fridge door real tight. Just slam it, girl. At's right."

He told me this every time I headed for the ancient white icebox housed behind the bar. Bottles of gaudy, outdated liqueurs stood in a line next to it: melon green Midori, bright red sloe gin, peach schnapps, dark brown creme de cacoa, which my cousin Theresa and I used to slam down, on the rocks, when we were teenagers—far too cool to participate in the raucous extended family Christmases.

We'd lean our bony limbs against the bar and talk languidly about boys, all the time refilling our low balls with liquor that had more in common with chocolate syrup than with booze. After a few prepatory shots, we'd add orange juice to create Tootsie Rolls, then sneak off to the bathroom to get drunk, squeeze blackheads, French braid our hair, and look at—for the millionth time—the illicit gizmo my Grandpa Pader had stashed up in his shaving kit. It was a small plastic figurine of a man and a woman, and when you pulled the string, they copulated. I remember the feeling of shame and embarrassment when I looked at it, and the strange mixture of disgust and curiosity that he'd own such a thing and have such thoughts.

I cracked open a beer, and waited for him to finish his exercise routine, but noticed something new. On the wall next to the bar was a large Rand McNally world map, pasted onto a huge slab of plywood. What surprised me was not so much the enormous size of the thing, but the fact that he had a map at all. He never had maps, even in the car, simply because he never went far enough to need one. He was born and raised in Hamburg, Minnesota, less than two miles away, and had lived the rest of his adult life in Green Isle, Minnesota, population 336. He referred to places by county, or even gravel roads, and had never been outside of Minnesota. He had an extremely small

Grandpa Pader,
Wilbert Gerhardt Panning

frame of reference for his world, and this bold new wall decoration intrigued me.

"So what's with the map?" I asked, and watched him dismount the machine, not without difficulty. His belly was so large it was worrisome. The bib of his overalls stretched over a stomach taut and awkward as a beach ball. It rode high on his body, and caused the small of his back to curve deeply inward; his shoulders reared back and left his arms dangling at the hips. Often he touched, caressed, patted, or massaged his large belly, as if there were a baby inside.

He walked up and knuckled the map; the plywood shook. "Yeah, good, kid, I meant to show you that. That's so I can keep track of you and that hubby of yours. I never know where the hell the two of you are. I'll see somebody when I'm up at the grocery, and they'll ask me where you live, I say don't know!" He was out of breath, but paused to drink down the last of his beer, crush the can, and stuff it in the back pocket of his overalls. He peered through his heavy glasses at the map, and traced a line with a thick, weather-worn finger. My eyes followed, and saw a shaky ball-point trail connecting Minnesota to the Philippines. "Yep, I got all the places you lived on here. Idaho, when you ran that crazy resort up there. Ohio, when you were getting more school. Got Hawaii. Got New York now where you're both professors, isn't that right?"

I nodded. He always asked me this as if he was unsure what it was my husband, Mark, and I actually did.

"That's pretty far away, huh? Your mom was over here one day and helped me with it. She sure is good to me, you know, always coming over and helping me clean and all. Because, kid, you know, ever since Myrt died, I just can't do for myself anymore. I just..."

He began to cry, without covering it up or apologizing. Little hot tears on such a large, old face: his glasses steamed. "I miss her so much," he said, voice cracking like a teenager's. He took a deep breath and stared out the window; I followed his gaze. A flat and empty Highway 12. Mailbox with the red flag down. Wispy new corn waving in the wind. Miles of dirt and rocks. The rain gauge, rusted.

"I know you miss her," I said. "It must be hard after so many years." I dared to touch his arm, then pulled back. "Wasn't it fifty years? Something like that?"

He nodded, but was lost in his stare. "Fifty-four years we were together when she died. Yeah." Finally, he wiped his eyes with his pinkies and clapped his hands, twice, fast. "Yeah, yeah, kid. Why don't you get us a couple more beers, we'll bring them upstairs. Christ, it's getting hotter than a son of a butch out there today." He pulled back the curtain, sighed, then chuckled. "But I suppose this is nothing compared to what you had in Hawaii, not so then?"

"Not so," I said, our old family way of expressing agreement. I gestured with my shoulder for him to follow me. "Let's go upstairs, okay?" With four cold cans of beer held against my chest, I dashed up the steps and wondered how much longer I should stay. I was home visiting for just a week while my husband, Mark, was making final revisions on his dissertation; I'd basically vacated to give him room and time to work without the danger of distractions. I'd come to Pader's house straight from the airport, and was tired. My parents' house was an easy seven miles away, my sister's house even less, but I decided to stick around a while longer. He seemed lonely.

My grandpa's name was not really Pader, but Wilbert Gerhardt Panning—100% German. 'Father' in German is 'pader,' and hearing my own father call him this for so many years had cemented the nickname. Whenever my parents hosted Christmas gatherings, he and my other grandfather, Henry Griep, would sit in the living room, palms on their knees, and converse in loud, slushy German—or what had transformed into their own hybrid version of it. Some words had stuck and become a permanent part of my own vocabulary, and when I eventually moved away and said things like, "Oh no, did you *verschulcht* yourself?" or "I've got a *rottsnauss*," or "*Machs nichts*," or "That *akles* me!" people were confused. They were not really German words anymore, but I found them hard to translate back into regular English.

My Grandpa Pader and I took our positions in the gigantic living room. He sat in the glider next to the candy dish, filled now with stale M&Ms and Brach's toffees, and I sat on the prim, uncomfortable couch. With his slight hearing problem, I had to shout across the cavern of space to be heard. They had built the house brand new from the ground up in 1983, a major improvement from the apartment they'd lived in above their general store, Panning's Town and Country. My Grandma Myrtle had wanted everything large and airy and capable of accommodating their three kids, eleven grandchildren, and seven great-grandchildren. She had insisted, in her tight-lipped, terse way, that the architects add an extra twelve feet to both the living room and the kitchen. As a result, the place felt like a community hall with rows and rows of cupboards in the kitchen, seating for at least twenty in the living room. Then she had died too early to enjoy any of it.

"So," I said, voice straining to be heard. "What's new around here these days? I see you've got the thermometer up and going." Mark had bought him a bright yellow John Deere thermometer last Christmas, and it was now nailed directly above the doorbell by the front door. Pader collected John Deere memorabilia like my little niece collected Disney. He had the caps, the calendars, the tractors, (both real and miniature), as well as the t-shirts, plaques, potholders, playing cards, mugs. He was a John Deere junkie, and when Mark showed up with the thermometer, I could see his brownie points as an in-law grandson escalating tenfold.

Pader's penchant for John Deere was not without history, though. When he was just seventeen, with an eighth-grade education, he had landed a much-coveted job at the Purina Feed Mill in town, which relied heavily on John Deere products and machinery. His girlfriend, my Grandma Myrtle, unmarried at the time and pregnant at sixteen, lived out in an old farmhouse and waited for him to get home every day, his John Deere cap and coveralls coated with a light layer of corn feed, obscuring the dark green logo. Maybe his love of John Deere had become a nostalgia for what it represented, for his move out of hard labor and into what eventually became their prosperous retail business. Maybe John Deere reminded him of his younger self. Maybe it reminded him of his life on the farm. Or, more likely than not, he simply loved farm machinery the way I loved office supplies: a sense of familiarity and hope in a blank page of heavy-weight, cotton-bond paper, the feeling of purpose and duty a fine-point, blue-ink Pentel provided, a certain peace realized with stacks of manila envelopes in the drawer, a sturdy Swingline stapler to punch together my pages. Good tools for honest work.

Pader finished off his beer, and I rose to get him another. I, too, was on my second, or third. "Not much new around here, kid," he said, and cracked it open. "What about you and Mark then? I suppose you're on your way to rich by now. You two are gonna make it big. That's what I always tell to your dad, too, when he comes over to cut my hair. I say, 'that Annie and Mark are going to have a load of money someday. With all that schooling they got.' Not so, huh? You'll be richer than me. Ha, ha, ha." He slapped his knee, gulped down some more beer, and regarded me with his head cocked, giving me his good ear.

Outside I could hear meadowlarks chirp in the fields. A faint breeze passed through the screen door, and for a moment, a large cloud mass covered the sun and colored the windows a dark, stormy gray. I thought I saw a funnel cloud take shape out on the horizon, but it seemed I was always imagining bad weather, even dreaming it up.

"I don't know, Pader. I don't think we'll ever be *rich*. Unfortunately they don't really pay you in academics for all the school you've had." No one in his family had ever gone to college—he had not even gone to high school, nor had my grandma. Neither of my parents had gone to college, nor had any of my siblings. Somehow I had latched onto the institution with a vengeance, though. I had found foreign languages there, travel, homosexual friends, Flannery O'Connor and John Cheever, drugs, boyfriends from other places, the thrilling pretense of the theatre, and how to live smart in a city, and safe. All of which, in retrospect, mainly served to alienate me, inevitably, from a family who didn't care a whit about these things. Although Pader, somehow, oddly did. In his own way, the death of his wife had opened up a space for him to communicate for the first time in years. He was able to shed his stoic, silent role, and come away animated, adept—an interested, entertaining conversationalist.

"So how's that Mark doing then?" Pader asked. We were still running through our stock gambit of questions, not to the good stuff yet. "He still a big boy?"

He was, he was, I said, but coming from 280-pound Pader, I had to laugh. Mark *was* a big boy, sort of: 6'4, 200 pounds, tall, long-limbed, and solid. Mark's size was to Pader's liking, though. He could swat him on the back, make him lift a box of cast-iron antiques just for the fun of it, laugh when Mark's head came precariously close to the ceiling in his shed. Their mutual bigness united them, fortunately, since Mark was an outsider, "not from around here," and needed any edge he could get. Bigness was something Pader could relate to, and he liked Mark best of all the in-law grandsons; you could tell.

"I sure do like that Mark," Pader said, and placed a wad of Copenhagen between his teeth and gum. "You want some?" he asked, and held out the tiny moist canister.

I shook my head.

"It's good shit," Pader said, and laughed. The gray sky was becoming darker, almost navy blue, and an earthy, wet smell blew through the curtains. The clocks ticked, all forty of them, then suddenly announced the hour noisily. They had been my Grandma Myrtle's collection, and ranged from a bright faux-brass sunburst to a wind-up Swiss chalet cuckoo to a wildlife wood duck framed in pine to an antique Coca-Cola from the old gas station in town. On the hour, and several minutes before and after, various chimes, dongs, and cheeps would echo throughout the house, absurd in their chaos, startling in their cacophony. Always, they made me think of my Grandma Myrtle, and often, not with fondness.

She had been as skinny, sharp, and pale as Pader was large, portly, and dark. She flew around the house like a hummingbird, never stopping to eat, always shoveling more hotdish onto my plate, hovering with fast wings above me, making me almost gorge myself on her fatty, fried meat, creamy egg pies, rich milk, and frozen ice cream desserts. Meanwhile, she'd sip at her blue plastic cup of coffee, no cream or sugar, and gaze down at me from the upper half of her bifocals. She had scared me, frankly, as a child, and in a sad guilty way, I did not miss her. Her death had given me a new grandfather—wonderfully fun and hilarious. But the memory of her manic love-hate relationship with me still resonated in the big, beautiful house she had left behind, well-decorated and preserved in a thousand shades of beige.

"I suppose you heard I got a new lady friend," Pader said, then tapped the top of his beer can nervously—waiting, I suppose, to see what I'd say.

"That's kind of what my dad was saying," I said, and ground my bare feet into the plush carpet. Actually, no one knew what exactly was going on in Pader's possible love life, so to be privy to this new information was an honor. My Grandma Myrtle had died a few years ago, so for this seventy-five year old widower to be dating again was a shock to the whole family. But in all fairness, I imagined he was ready. He had nursed my grandma through a long, laborious, seven-year disease, and as much as he still loved her, she had truly left him years prior. He had wiped her after going to the bathroom, washed her armpits with a soft, pink cloth, pulled loose dresses over her shaky arms, pushed her around in her wheelchair, even spoke for her. Towards the end, Pader would try to feed her Ensure, but it ended up dribbling down her mouth and chin and blouse—a watery chocolate mess. She had lost all control, and it had broken Pader's heart to witness this, day after difficult day.

Before I could inquire further about his new "lady friend," Pader suggested we go outside to check on the weather. "I just want to get a look south-south-west to make sure there's no storm brewing out there." But I figured he was also embarrassed, somewhat, about his revelation.

"Sure," I said, and followed him out the front door. He lived on an acre and a half of fertile land, surrounded by cornfields on three sides and a gravel road on the other. The sky was his dome, and he could spot storms approaching when they were literally two towns away. His front yard was void of trees, except for two twin sugar maples, tiny and choked around the necks with black "training" wires, so they could withstand the heavy winds that ripped through the open plains. He had a bright white strip of sidewalk out front, free of stains, that led to the garage and to the shed out back.

"Hey kid, have you seen my new wheels?" He stood in the middle of the lawn, hands on hips, gazing at the sky. The air was humid but suddenly cool. A thick band of slate gray hung over a thicker band of blue-black, like a charcoal smudge. I actually shivered, and this cracked Pader up. "It must be seventy-eight degrees hot outside and you're shivering, kid. That's a good one!"

"I can't help it," I said. "It looks like it's gonna rain." The sky rumbled. From where I stood, I could see only two other clusters of farms. Both were designed with windbreaks of poplar and evergreens protecting them in perfect, straight rows, and consisted of red barns, silver silos, white two-story farmhouses, and various, dilapidated storage sheds, peeling paint.

Pader took one last scan of the sky, doing a 360, a slow shuffle dance with heavy feet. "Yeah, yeah. Why don't you come and take a look at my car then? I traded in the the Astrovan now that Mryt don't need to ride around in it anymore with her wheelchair." We walked down the skinny sidewalk and he rolled up the garage door. Inside stood a navy blue late model Chrysler Towne Car. Silver spokes glittered inside the hub cabs. Next to it stood his little white truck, which was only used for ice fishing, hauling things to the dump, and picking up fertilizer for the lawn.

"Wow," I said, and ran my hand over it. The top was soft and hard at the same time, like clay. "Pretty nice." I tried to feign excitement, but he seemed to be getting a new, different luxury car every other year, and they all looked the same with only slight variations: navy blue, burgundy, dark green; Grand Marquee, Towne Car, LeBaron; electric windows, automatic antennae, tinted windows. The only times these "good" cars ever got used was for Sunday church services, golden anniversary parties, funerals, or appointments at the bank.

Pader opened the door of the car and told me to get in, to see how it felt. "Just sit down on those plush seats and you can see what a great car I've got myself here." I obeyed. The door was ajar; the buzzer sounded as I sat there, hands on the wheel, body enveloped in seats softer and more comfortable than my own couch at home. Pader stood with his elbow on the door, smiling like a kid. "Pretty nice, huh?"

I looked through the windshield and saw the old cash register from their store, a tall, curlicued antique with round, high-stemmed keys, sitting on a shelf. Duckshit green waders hung off a nail, and a bubbling Hamm's beer sign was propped up against a bright blue ice auger. I wondered if he took his "lady friend" out on dates in this good

car, or if she was relegated to the little white truck, and decided I would have to dig for more information.

"So, Pader," I asked, still inside the car. "Tell me about your new friend. How did you meet her?"

"Yeah, just a minute. You want another beer?"

I nodded. Luckily, there was a fridge in the garage, an old-fashioned one with only one door and a tiny metal box inside for a freezer. He handed me a Milwaukee's Best, but before opening it, ducked outside to get another look at the weather.

"Still looks thick out there. Could rain," he said, and pulled open a lawnchair. The nylon webbing sagged deeply under the pressure of his body, but did not give. "Maybe you should stick around in case a tornado comes up. We can just run for the basement if we need, not so?"

I glanced in the rearview mirror and saw a rectangle of sick, dark sky, though it was only mid-afternoon. 5:14, to be exact, since my Grandma Myrtle had not forgotten to place one of her famous clocks in the garage. This was a simple black and white schoolhouse clock with a bright red second hand. "Yeah, I suppose we should keep an eye on it," I said. "So, you were just going to tell me about..."

"Yeah, yeah, kid. Her name's Esther Trebelhorn from Winthrop," he said, and pronounced it "Win-trop," a small farm town fifteen miles away. He hiked up the legs of his overalls and rested the beer can on one knee. "Her husband passed away about three and a half years ago. Real nice lady. Real friendly. I went to school with her when we were kids." He sipped his beer.

"How did you meet her?"

"Golden wedding anniversary dance in Arlington. She's about two years younger than me, and we get ourselves to lots of dances together. She loves to dance and so do I. But you know that, kid, not so?"

I did. When Mark and I got married, Pader and I had flown across the lawn under the stars to an upbeat double-time polka. With his hand firmly planted on the small of my back, he had kept us revolving in a tightly controlled spiral, all the time leaping off his toes and kicking back his heels with the energy and speed of a cheerleader. His smell that night of sweat, pipe tobacco, and Old Spice still lingered in my mind.

"That's great," I said. "It's nice to have company as you get older." I placed my beer in the cup holder between the seats.

Pader seemed puzzled for a moment, or uncertain, then leaned closer toward the car and said, "Just between you and me, kid, I don't know that I'm ready for this. You see, she's not skinny and pretty like Myrtle. And you see, well, that's costing me a lot of money to go out to these dances. You gotta pay the five dollar ticket for admittance, and I'm the one's gotta pay for hers, too, since she's the lady, not so?"

"I guess so," I said.

"And you gotta buy her a nice drink, too, only it's good because Esther drinks beer and that's the cheapest." He drank down some of his own and wiped his mouth. "Then you gotta pay for gas in the car for all that running back and forth between here to Winthrop. It all adds up, is what I'm saying, kid. I just don't know if I can keep up with it. I'm gonna go broke if I do."

I wanted to say, "Hardly!" but instead said, "Well, do you like her? I mean, do you value her company?"

He nodded, and looked at me imploringly, as if I might tell him the right thing to do. What I thought he probably wanted was permission and reassurance that it was okay to see someone else after my grandmother had died, and I wanted to give that to him, but didn't quite know how. Oddly after all these years of his inquiries about my boyfriends and relationships, the tables were turned. I felt like the grown-up.

"Well, she sounds nice," I said. "And as long as you're happy, that's the most important thing."

"Well," he said, "I don't know that I'll ever be happy again." He tapped a finger on his beer can and finished it.

"Pader," I said. "You shouldn't..."

"Let's go outside," he said. "Check on that weather and maybe get you on your way."

I followed him outside, where it had just began to rain—small, clear drops that darkened the sidewalk gradually and almost seemed to sizzle. I let myself get wet, until Pader beckoned me toward the house.

"Maybe you should stay here until this passes," he said, standing under the eave of the front door, dry.

A jagged flash of lightning lit up the sky far off, and I started counting: 1, 2, 3, 4, 5, 6, 7: thunder. The sound made my whole body relax and feel at home. I hadn't realized how much I'd missed the Midwest until standing right there, in the middle of his huge lawn while it began to pour. Everything smelled fresh and ripe and alive. The gray sky felt large and inviting, and being in the middle of all that space cleared my head in a way it never cleared in New York. I felt I had my legs again, and stood firmly on land that at one point I never thought I'd leave.

"I have to go, Pader," I said. "I told my mom I'd be there for dinner. She'll be worried if it starts to storm and I'm out driving."

"Wait until the storm passes," he said, half inside the door.

"No, I like storms," I said. "Especially driving in them." I jingled the keys in my hand.

He laughed. "You and that Mark. You both like that crazy weather, not so?"

I nodded, ran up to the door, and hugged him briefly. His stomach stood between us like a third body. "I'll call you before I head back to New York!" I shouted, running to my rental car and quickly rolling up all the windows. I waved and blew Pader a kiss as I pulled out of his long, horseshoe driveway. He waved back from behind the screen door, and, unintentionally, I kicked up some gravel as I pulled out onto the highway.

The road was slick and deserted, and rain sprayed at me from all sides. Inside, I was damp and chilly, but the interior of the car felt cozy and small, private and safe. The windows fogged; the radio played an eighties flashback; the sight of the familiar sky blue water tower comforted me up ahead. I could hear my own breathing. A large semi-truck blasted past me, but the car remained steady. The windshield wipers worked furiously; I could sense the road curving, arching around Brooke's dairy farm, and I knew I was almost home. I thought of Pader again, his feet firmly planted on the ground, his thick German accent I could hear like no other in my head, his dim form behind the screen door, clouded by sheets of rain. For better or worse, he was grounded in a way I knew I wasn't, might never be.

I knew there were multiple valid and important reasons I'd left the Midwest back when I was just twenty-one years old, but as I drove the final stretch of Highway 5 through lightning and thunder, past the new Food 'n Fuel, past the bowling alley, down Main Street which contained a single stoplight swaying in the wind, none of them seemed clear anymore; none of them had led me to a home as permanent as this one. My Grandpa Pader, of course, and all my relatives, had stuck it out, while I had wandered place after place, searching. ◆●◆

© Susanna Sharp-Schwacke, 2006

FOR A JUNKIE SHOOTING UP

KEN MEISEL

Once, when there was nothing
left in the sky but big clouds,
and a rainfall that was just starting
to spit, I saw a woman shooting
up, scoring before nightfall,
in the rough edge of a field
where there used to be a building.
She was part animal now,
and part orphan, as if she'd once
belonged to somebody, but not
any more. Now she belonged to
whatever it is takes a body out,
past the spotlight of common
sense and decency, and into
whatever it is becomes of somebody seeping like backwash, away.
If you were a novelist, you'd
note in the scene that a person
committing suicide by injection
refuses to acknowledge her
creator, you, and so you'd feel
the guttural emptiness that addiction
or loneliness always brings.
If you were a pulp fiction writer
you'd give her a black eye,
and a backside of scars. And a pimp
lurking behind her like charcoal.
And if you were a talking head
you'd discuss socio-economic
reasons for why it is she's frothing
at the mouth and bleeding
for the sake of societal problems,
and opportunities dried up.

If you were a painter brushing
this scene into truthfulness,
you'd add the white ghosting
of malevolent death stalking
her like a cloudy shadow. And if you
were Gordon Parks, the photographer,
you'd paste in a picture
of her anguished grandmother,
tears like streams of mercury
rolling down her dark crinkled face.
The five year old daughter
peering bashfully at the camera,
another child of the State.
And if you were Chirico, you'd see
there was a dog, too. It roamed
uneasily past the corner party
store and down, beyond the
apartment buildings, as if searching
for somebody lost. If you were
a poet describing what you saw,
you'd invent a word for people
being consumed by leprosy
of the soul. It would have to rhyme
with awe but not belong
to God or the Devil, but rather
to the negotiation in between light
and sadness, where the beings
who've not yet decided who they
belong to, truly live. Not ghosts,
you'd have to point out,
so much as those in between
ghosts and the living forgetables.
Those that wild dogs smell.
Long before the morning comes.

SIGNS
ALAN S. AMBRISCO

Strange, how she never smelled bad
When she came from the horses each night.

It must have been love, I thought,
but as the years went by,
I figured it was allergies.

How much time do we spend
wondering what we think,
looking for signs in the sky?

Sometimes, what we think
is little more than neurons firing
at random, dice playing God with the universe

while fate, trapped in teacups and viscera,
flails around the world,
time to kill, looking for a barstool.

The real mysteries happen beneath
the skin, cool to the touch, threaded
with desire, bolted down with pain.

SNAPSHOT
ALAN S. AMBRISCO

In New Harmony, Indiana,
I saw a hawk in flight so still
it hurt, stripped to bare essentials,
action and repose,
wings long and level,
head stretched like a racehorse.
I shifted below, gathering it in,
all Kodak and Technicolor,
finger poised on the button
to hold in check the ruffled finery
of the world, until I put the camera down,
stretched my arms wide in the wind
and felt a rush of air lift me, too.

MONA'S EAGLE
LAURA ELIZABETH PEARSON

Eagle
  Majestic bird of the sky
    Brought down from your lofty flight
     Wounded
       By power lines strung from pole to pole
       Near death you lay
        Cold in marshy waters
         Feathers picked by hungry crows
         Lifted up by those who dare
        To care for all of life.

Eagle
  Majestic bird of the sky
    Now you sit on tethered perch
     With sightless eyes
       You scan with hearing keen
        Head moving in minute and subtle ways
        Waiting
         Without judgment
          For what will come.

Eagle
  Majestic bird of the sky
    You cannot know
     The lesson you have brought
       To all of those who honor and observe
       That nature holds no judgment.
        Eagle
         With your sightless eyes
          You have given us a gift.

BACK TO THE WILD
MONA RUTGER, DIRECTOR, BACK TO THE WILD

IN THE BEGINNING!

The most often asked question by visitors at Back to the Wild and by students attending programs is "How and what made you ever get started in this?" I'm not sure if I can truly answer this question, because I believe "it" found "me." Here's my story:

Back to the Wild began in our backyard, in the spring of 1990. Without ever having really planned this new chapter in my life, I suddenly found myself unwilling to continue my job status of 22 years as a secretary. I began developing an overwhelming desire to spend more time out of doors where I could observe and explore the birds, insects, wildflowers and trees that I loved so much! Changing gears completely, I was surprised to find myself hired by the local Metroparks as a seasonal naturalist where I spent the next several summers teaching children about nature. Another few years were spent working for the Ohio Division of Wildlife, National Wildlife Research Center and as a volunteer for local State Nature Preserves. There was no turning back! With my two children quickly approaching high school and college age and becoming quite independent, I began entertaining the idea that I could try to do something about a problem that had been apparent to me for a long time. What could be done to help the wildlife that was being so *severely* affected by human carelessness? What could I do, on a *personal* basis, to make a differ-

© Becky Dickerson, 2006

ence—to help people understand how imperative it is to stop allowing habitat destruction? I desperately felt I had to do something! I took some steps toward that goal, but little did I know where they would take me!

I spent the winter months of 1990, researching, learning and obtaining necessary State and Federal permits that would allow me to possess and care for injured and orphaned wildlife. Those months of preparation resulted in a small clinic area in our own new barn, which we had just proudly built. It would be a wonderful, needed addition to our ten acres my husband and I had been restoring to wildlife habitat for the past 16 years. The original purpose of that barn was for our personal needs (storing our tractor, mower, tools and maybe even a car). My hesitant, but wonderfully supportive, husband knew I was determined and willingly sacrificed a portion of his barn to my new life's work. Quietly at first, a few make-shift, home-made cages and incubators and an old freezer began lining the walls and I felt quite confidant I was "ready" to begin my life as a wildlife rehabilitator. (I thought my modest little clinic was quite complete!)

During those first few weeks of spring and summer, numerous helpless, orphaned and injured wild animals arrived at a surprisingly steady rate—more than I had anticipated, but I just added a few cages, scavenging anything I could find. By fall, I was amazed at the numbers of wild creatures who had found their way to our home. It seemed word had gotten out fast that there finally was a place licensed to accept injured wildlife. Up to that point, people had nowhere to go when they encountered an injured or displaced wild animal, and without permits, they could not raise or care for wildlife themselves and there just were no facilities in the area. That first year of rehabilitation, I treated 54 wild animals. By winter, when things slowed down, I knew I had to plan for some additions and changes to better accommodate next year's arrivals. In fact, I began dreaming of some wonderful outdoor, large cages that would become naturalized homes for recovering animal patients. I knew I needed one special cage—*a raptor flight cage*—to con-

Mona Rutger and friend.

dition and prepare large birds of prey for their release back into the wild. This cage was not just something I wanted, it was mandatory by Federal and State regulations. I was excited to have this structure become part of my little wildlife center.

GROWING—AND GROWING!

By the spring of 1991, preparations for the new flight cage had begun. Forty-eight utility poles had been collected; and, with a small army of *brave* volunteers, some borrowed scaffolding, lots of plywood, and rolls of expensive avian netting, we began to build. (My husband was slowly, unknowingly becoming my partner in crime! I'll admit—we were hooked!) Sinking 48 utility poles 4' in the ground, to reach a 16' high roof, was a real feat! Fields were impossibly wet in March and just about every tractor, truck and vehicle became stuck at some point. What a month *that* was! I can hardly believe that most

© Becky Dickerson, 2006

of those original volunteers are still with us after putting them through that! Our funding was non-existent, so this strange looking assortment of phone poles sticking out of the ground just stood there for the next several months. (One observer commented that it looked like Stonehenge!) What must the neighbors be saying?

Meanwhile, injured and orphaned animals continued to arrive in *shocking* numbers—triple that of the previous year—and I was spending long hours trying to keep up. My work area in our barn began consuming more walls and an aisle of cages slowly grew down the middle. Two more freezers were added! The mower sat outside and no cars *ever* entered the barn again! A very tolerant husband shared the larger portion of his barn with my work as it was quickly overtaken by the needs of the center. Mid-summer, a little duckling arrived. Its human owners wanted it to return to the wild. They were truly animal lovers and spent lots of time talking to us about what we were doing to help wildlife. They saw an assortment of ducks, geese, baby foxes, squirrels, a bobcat and a few hawks and owls. When I explained our plans for the partially built flight cage, they asked what it

would take to finish it. "A couple of thousand dollars worth of treated lumber," I replied, and realized its completion would be a long way off.

© Becky Dickerson, 2006

The gentleman said, "Your lumber will be here tomorrow morning by 10:00 a.m." That was our turning point. *A donor—a supporter— had arrived and help was on the way!* These generous animal lovers lived up to their word. That summer, several volunteers helped to build our flight cage. Once again I thought my center was just about complete!

By the end of summer, I began to realize one flight cage was just not enough. It was always occupied and I had "patients" waiting. Because species couldn't be mixed, plans were soon underway for a second large flight cage. Things were changing fast. That second winter, more and more plans developed. Visitors began pouring in to learn about the center. Teachers and youth leaders began requesting tours and I knew there was a tremendous opportunity to use this activity as a way to educate children especially, about our wonderful native wildlife and the natural world. The following spring, over 500 school children visited my center for educational field trips. That same spring, my wildlife patients jumped to over 800 individuals!

I'm not sure when it happened, but at some point, Back to the Wild took on a life of its own and consumed mine with it! In just 15 years, we have built 32 outside cages to accommodate over 2,200 wild animals admitted each year and have put in an amphitheater to seat over 120 school children! Several thousand children and adults now visit the center annually to attend educational programs. Back to the Wild presented programs to over 53,000 students and members of youth groups and adult organizations at schools, churches, summer camps and libraries last year! Our property has grown to 30 acres, including 18 wooded acres. We have gone from no electricity in the

© Becky Dickerson, 2006

barn or cages (wearing a miner's lamp on my head to do my work at night) to several well-lit cages and two large barns. The stone floor in our barn became a concrete floor and after years of hauling water buckets long distances, new water lines were run to the barn and cage. But by 1997, my wildlife center had simply outgrown the barn. It just wasn't fair to take it away from our personal use and needs.

Dreaming a Building—Building a Dream!

I dreamed of a building . . . just for Back to the Wild! We desperately needed a much larger clinic area and added shelter for animal patients during severe weather conditions. I needed an office to keep the large volumes of traffic and paperwork out of my home, and a place to house all the educational materials and displays used for programs. And we needed a solution for school field trips that often had to be canceled due to rainy days—an *indoor* classroom! Was I asking too much? Admittedly, I thought I surely was. But if I could build this addition to the center, maybe then I could say, "*Now my wildlife center is complete!*"

It's Happened! It's Here!

Bck to the Wild finally has a building of its own! Several years of fund-raisers have helped us to realize this dream! Even though we took out a huge personal loan to begin construction of this new building, it wouldn't have been possible to make the leap, without the generosity and support of several local foundations, businesses and individuals who have contributed to make this building a reality! There have been so many people in the community who have given their financial support, time and labor for the past several years, to help construct this building and to benefit wildlife here at the center! Back to the Wild is able to continue to exist and improve its efforts in wildlife rehabilitation and education because of the generosity and support of many caring individuals!

My work in wildlife rehabilitation is truly a "labor of love" and I want to share it with anyone who will listen. I want to help children, especially, learn to respect, appreciate, preserve, and protect our natural world and

help them become responsible caretakers of the earth, and to understand our own inter-connection with all living things. I love to watch children discover the wonders of nature and I feel privileged and honored to be a part of that process.

In the beginning, I wanted to do what I could to help wild animals, but these animals who have come through the center, whom I have held in my hands and spent countless hours healing and worrying over, and who have allowed me to share just a brief moment in their wild lives—have given me more than I ever have been able to give them. They have given me the gifts of compassion, respect, understanding, and completeness. ◆•◆

Muggsy Donovan at the Library
Andrew W. Grossman

Muggsy Donovan rarely visited our local library...

His given name was Robert but we all called him Muggsy because he looked like a really ugly bassett hound with a pushed-in nose and chunky stature.

He never read anything unless Mr. Gordon, our fourth grade teacher insisted on it, and called on him in class. It's not that he could not read. I remember that he once stood in front of our class and did an excellent job reading a passage from Hawthorne. He just hated reading and we could not understand why that was so.

Then one Friday afternoon at recess in early December Jerry White, another classmate whom we called Doodles because he liked to draw, told me about the 'Dirty' books he had found at the library, in the adult section. It was very cold outside that day, but the sun was out and the skies were exceptionally blue and clear of clouds. So the teachers allowed all the kids to go outside and get some air. They probably needed a little break from us.

I asked Jerry how he found these books. It turned out that whenever his mom or dad went to the library, they dragged him with them. The good thing about it was that with either parent there he could enter the adults room and the librarian could not stop him. Otherwise she would shoo him out of the room and 'encourage' him to go to the children's room where she was certain he belonged.

One fine Saturday while his dad read some business magazine, Jerry was wandering around the medical section and hit upon the gold mine. "You have got to get in there and see these pictures," he uttered excitedly. I have to admit I was curious.

That was easier said than done. My father owned a warehouse and clothing store. He was always busy. His idea of reading was to pick up the newspaper when he came home, and read it cover to cover. My mother simply had no interest in anything other than raising her children, working part time, and spending as much time with her millions of cousins and other sundry friends.

If I were to see this treasure, I would have to do it on my own.

I noticed Muggsy standing about ten feet away from us while Jerry described the stacks in the adult section where I could find the forbidden treasure. Neither of us took particular notice of him, and Jerry thought he was whispering to me. With Jerry a whisper was like a train whistle. You can hear it clearly for miles around. I'm surprised the teachers didn't hear him. Perhaps they had collapsed, or were paralyzed by exhaustion.

"The best thing about it is if you get back there without the Old Crow seeing you, she can't see that row from her desk."

The "Old Crow" was Miss Norris, the librarian. A tougher, more rigid woman never existed. She was like the Devil himself, except she wore black and grey dresses, not red. Not even red lipstick; somehow we fourth grade boys noticed that. Occasionally, we expected to see a forked tail stick out from underneath her long plain skirts.

Miss Norris was tall and painfully thin. She wore her hair in a bun as if she were back in the 1890's. It still reminds me of a large pile of horse manure, resting precariously on top of her head.

It never occurred to us that she might be married and have a zillion children of her own. We were convinced that Miss Norris was a sour old prune who had never experienced the pleasures of a man. The thought that she may have experienced the pleasures of another woman did not cross our minds. Besides, as nine year olds we were not that creative.

No, Miss Norris was a single woman, without children, and no prospects for the softness and caresses of love. Which made us all wonder how she knew us all so well. We could not help notice that she was always there ready to pounce on us the minute we stepped out of line. It was as if she had x-ray vision — like Superman — and could spy on us right through the massive piles of books and other material in the huge room.

Take, for example, the time earlier that year when Brian Garrett and Jimmie Olsen decided to sabotage the drinking fountain, just to get her for throwing them out a week earlier. They admitted making too much noise. They even apologized to her. Yet she called their mothers, and the principal, Mr. Provost.

Brian's father was a psychiatrist so he had to sit through hours of nauseating lectures about his own psyche, and penis envy, and God knows what else. Jimmie, on the other hand, heard her mother say the dread words, "Wait till your father gets home!" And his father, the owner of a successful specialty steel warehouse, was one of those no-nonsense fathers. Without a word he took out his cane and whacked Jimmie on the behind twice. He would have hit him one more time except Mom stepped in and said, "That's enough, Clyde." So Clyde stopped.

The next afternoon, a Saturday, they met at the old Cedar Avenue movie house. The two of them sat all the way in the back and plotted their revenge on Miss Norris.

It was really a simple plan. They watched Miss Norris for the better part of a week and noticed that almost every hour, on the hour, she trotted her skinny self over to the drinking fountain and took a long drink of water.

Thursday was the appointed hour at which to strike a blow for boyhood against the malevolent librarian who controlled so much of their lives. Jimmie's mother sewed dresses. He snatched one of her dress pins. "She won't miss it," he argued. "She has a million of them."

They waited until Miss Norris went to the assistance of an elderly patron at the other end of the room, then shoved the pin down into the drinking fountain's tap. Brian tested it. It worked superbly. A huge geyser of water issued forth and landed about ten feet from where they stood. Satisfied with their efforts, the two boys went to a table in the children's room where they were certain to see the results of their plan.

It was too bad they ignored the puddle that lay on the hard tile floor, not too far from the front door. They hadn't prepared for such a long hard spray.

The two boys fixed on Miss Norris's face as she returned to her post at the front desk. She noticed them. A quizzical expression crossed her sharp china blue eyes. Placing a few books on the desk she crossed the short distance to the water fountain at about the same time that Mayor Crosby entered the room.

At almost the exact moment she leaned over to drink, and he stepped on the puddle. In an almost perfectly synchronized ballet, water shot out of the fountain and hit Miss Norris in the face, while the mayor's feet shot out from under him and flipped high into the air.

Miss Norris reacted with red rage, straightening like a walking staff, while the mayor landed on his posterior, arms flailing to and fro.

The two boys froze in their chairs, a look of disbelief and horror plastered on their little faces. Miss Norris turned to face the room. As water dripped from her face, and down the blouse of her dress, she used an arm to wipe it out of her eyes.

The next thing she saw, to her dismay, was the mayor, lying on the floor in front of her, groaning magnificently, like a big, beached whale. She took off her rimless eyeglasses and stared right at the boys, that death ray stare clawed into their brains and read their thoughts. Brian and Jimmie were instantly trapped.

I was determined to get past the intrepid dreadnaught who guarded the morals of the town's youth from her battleship at the front desk. I had to see the photographs in those books for myself. Remembering the experience of my two friends, I sat down to think of a way to get past the guardian of community morals without being seen. All I would have needed was to be caught by Norris and my parents would punish me severely, not to mention what Miss Norris might do.

Back in those halcyon days a parent could hit a child almost at will. Adults, in general, such as teachers, could punish you rather badly. Children were not paid much attention until they screwed up. I certainly had no intention to get caught looking at forbidden material. My dad would skewer me, and that was after my mother got through with me. Jewish women are a lot like Hungarian and Italian women. They know how to pull guilt strings. Since my mother was both Hungarian and Jewish, I would get a double whammy if caught by the wicked Miss Norris.

I had no real plan that Saturday afternoon. I simply loped into the library with my fingers crossed in my pockets and said, "Hello" to the Wicked Witch of the West. I was keyed up as I meandered into the Children's Room. She ignored me as she sat working at her desk. Her long sharp nose was buried in stacks of catalog cards. She barely looked up to acknowledge my presence and went right back to the cards, a sharp pencil in one hand.

The old library building was built during the Great Depression, in 1933 or 1934. Its outside façade was composed of brown brick. Sanded gray granite slabs surrounded each window, which was painted a standard yellow enamel, mixed with lead. When you entered the building through the front door the offices were just to your left.

The long main checkout desk stood directly in front of the main doors. The Children's Room was off to the right and directly ahead, behind the main desk. It was a long narrow room; material for the younger children was stored closest to the main desk. The books for older children were farther back. They took up more than half the room, and were housed on standard library shelves, six deep. Whoever was at the main desk could swivel her head to the left and look down through the stacks to ensure that there was no (usually male) hanky-panky in the room.

If you turned into the room to your left, you entered the reference room. An avuncular reference librarian sat behind the reference desk, reading the latest volume of the Oxford English Dictionary. He was so skinny, not to mention pimply and tall, that he gave the appearance of a lost stork. It was accentuated by the tiny desk behind which he sat. It was further exaggerated by the fact that his large bony knees stuck out from behind the desk in an awkward manner.

I entered through the main door and walked past the restrooms, on either side, into the main area. I carried a school book and pad of writing paper. I looked the part of a dutiful student about to embark on a scholarly adventure.

In order to get into the adult room you had to pass through the reference room, which meant you had to get past two guardians of decency and the secrets of adulthood. Getting past Miss Norris was a breeze. She was too busy fighting her way through a mass of little cards and ledger-like books.

The "Stork" was another story.

I turned into the reference area and kept walking until I found myself behind the long man in the little swivel seat. He never surrendered his focus on the book he diligently studied. I was beyond the landmines and headed for the adult room.

Until I caught a flower pattern at the very edge of my right eye, and turned my head, briefly. Miss Norris was on the move. As she headed straight toward me I moved sideways, like a crab, until I stood in front of the *Encyclopedia Britannica* stack, and pretended to hunt for a particular letter.

Miss Norris made a sharp right turn into the adult room. I was compelled to follow at a distance as if she was a giant horseshoe magnet, and I was an iron nail. It was during this short trip into infamy that I noticed what a wide ass she had under her long flower print dress. I watched her butt swing from side to side with such concentration that I nearly crashed into her when she stopped abruptly at the head of an aisle.

"Arthur Robert Donovan!" she snapped in a vicious voice, like the crack of a whip. "What do you think you are doing?" It caused old Mr. Peckinpaugh to look up from the newspaper he was reading. But he just smiled a knowing smile and went on reading his paper.

From clear down the other end of the row I heard, "Nothing, Aunt Ida," in a quavering tremulous tone.

"Get over here now! And bring that book with you." Another crack of the whip from Miss Norris.

I almost missed the "Aunt Ida" part, but my mind caught up with my ears. So Muggsy had two secrets that he did not want to share with the rest of us. The second one was his first name: Arthur! He obviously hated it. Otherwise, he would have proudly informed us of it.

I sat down at a nearby table and spread my books out as if I were studying. A hidden blade of glee permeated my brain as I pretended not to notice the librarian and her nephew.

When Arthur emerged from the aisle between the two tall stacks, he was holding a medical text with illustrations. Old Needle Nose grabbed the book out of his hands and marched him right past me to the front desk and certain death, or worse. When Muggsy spotted me, he blushed deeply, reminding me of a ripe peach. He

knew he was screwed, that I would tell all the boys what his real first name was.

Old Mr. Peckinpaugh never stirred from reading his newspaper. He just smiled, a secret of his own hiding behind those wrinkled hooded eyelids.

At that very moment I was more interested in what other treasures lay in wait at the end of the forbidden aisle of medical texts. So, glancing at the old man in the armchair not twenty feet from where I sat, I waited until Miss Norris was around the corner in the reference room and made a dash between the stacks.

I began to browse the titles on the ends of the book jackets until I found a likely looking title: "Gray's Anatomy." I had never heard of it before. As I reached for it I heard a throat clear behind me. "Ahem."

I froze where I stood. Then I heard the dreadful, high-pitched, scornful voice of Miss Norris.

"Mr. Roth. What are you doing?"

There was no use thinking up an excuse. I suppose I could have told her I had a science assignment, which was true. She knew what it was. All of the teachers gave the librarian copies of their class assignments, and she knew my teacher. She read and always memorized them as if they were religious tracts.

Although she was required to keep them on file, she never seemed to refer to them. "Oh, yes," Miss Norris would chant, like a Gregorian-era monk. "I set aside references and books for Mrs. Stein's class right over here." She would lead the way to a particular bookshelf in the Children's Room and point out the material. There was no need to go anywhere else after that.

"I was just curious about why Mug… err… Arthur was in trouble," I explained.

"I see," she replied, leaning over to face me, her long, sharp, needle nose not an inch from mine. I wanted to punch it, hard. "I think you ought to go back to where you belong and take your books with you." Our elders were very big on the concept of your place in the universe. The evil Miss Norris was a great one for upholding the rules.

"Yes ma'am," I said, and headed back to the Children's Room, where I found Muggsy sitting at the table nearest the checkout desk.

I never did reveal Muggsy's real first name…that is, until now. ◆●◆

THE CLASS POETS: A PROFILE
COMPILED BY LARRY SMITH, MANAGING EDITOR

"Class Poets"—that title may echo for you as it does me. A million of us must be out there, for each class has one or several nowadays. You know, the writer in the class, the one who is driven by a need for expression, a love of words, and an intensity of feeling. They often begin by writing poems in diaries kept in desk drawers, then they begin sharing them with friends, eventually writing them for and about those friends. Ultimately they read those poems at coffeehouses, post them around school, publish them in local magazines, write the class song or poem. It's a gift that only works if you give it away. Some will never let it go ("I write because I have to") and go on to write and publish books of poems for a larger audience, but none so sweet as loved ones and classmates. We share with you here some of our area's Class Poets.

EMILY MASTROIANNI
12th Grade Graduate,
Monroeville High School, Monroeville, OH

BIOGRAPHICAL STATEMENT: I will be attending Baldwin-Wallace College in the fall to study psychology and minor in theatre. I have a passion for the performing arts; acting, singing, and dancing, and I love all genres of music. I live with my mom, dad, younger brother and my dog, Anchor. My family, friends, and faith are most important to me and drive me to be the best everyday.

WRITING STATEMENT: I write to express myself and say what I can't say out loud. I find more power with a pen in my hand sometimes and I let it drain me of my crazy emotions. Writing helps me organize my thoughts and sometimes turns the mess in my head into something beautiful on paper. I've been keeping a journal since first grade and have learned first hand how valuable and soothing writing can be.

CINDERELLA SYNDROME
EMILY MASTROIANNI

I'm so good at this
Building myself up for the fall
Training my mind and heart
To believe in make believe
Trade in all common sense
For a fairy tale gown
And glass slippers
Only to have them disappear
At midnight
When I'm stunned back into reality
As I hold these rags you left with me
Taking all the magic for yourself
Looking so innocent
So nonchalant
As if you knew this is how it would end
All in a day's work
Maybe it was my mistake
I must of been dreaming
Sorry now you disturbed my sleep
Please let me rest in peace
It was so much easier when I had no wishes

No bit of you to linger in my mind
But I'll keep doing this
Building castles in the sand
Waiting for high tide to whisk them away
I wish the sea would take me too
So I could float away from here
Scatter these broken pieces of my heart
They are of no use to me anymore
Stopped feeling long ago
Or maybe I'll place them in a bottle
To be tossed to the waves
Hoping one day someone will return them saying,
"I found these pieces.
Such a beautiful thing so carelessly thrown away
It took all my love to mend it,
But here it is..."
And he'll place my heart back into my hands
Whole
And I'll hand it back with a smile,
"No, you keep it now...
It's yours."

AMANDA THEIS

(12TH GRADE, SENECA EAST HIGH SCHOOL; REPUBLIC, OH)

BIOGRAPHICAL STATEMENT: I live in Republic, in the country. In school I do volleyball, basketball, and track. I am also in the National Honor Society, Yearbook staff, Pep Club, boy's basketball stats, and an Ohio Reads Mentor. All of those things are important to me, and I take pride them, as I do my family, friends, and faith.

WRITING STATEMENT: I write because it's a form of freedom to me. The freedom to express my feelings in the form of writing. It makes me feel free in that I am able to express my thoughts and not keep them locked inside.

TO STRIVE FOR INDIVIDUALISM
AMANDA THEIS

Deep insecurities flood my eyes
Some days it feels as if they are judged
Others they feel deeply hidden
One wish is to have none to worry me,
Nothing to disclose,
That would be a great relief
No secrets, the real me
The world is an easy place for frauds
If no one knows the strange me
No one can dislike me
In this mixed up home
There are fakes surrounding,

Encompassing so much,
It's simple to be caught up
Attitudes as if I was shunned
I will conform
This is the golden rule for acceptance,
But not the secret to genuine beings
It's time for individualism
There is a deep need for sincere compassion
Not momentary acceptance or love
God deserves all our focus and dedication
In order for uniqueness
True human uniqueness where no one is replicated

SHELBY TINMAN

(10TH GRADE MONROEVILLE HIGH SCHOOL; MONROEVILLE, OH)

BIOGRAPHICAL STATEMENT: I live on a farm where I raise rabbits and sheep; I also have a few cats and dogs. I participate in 4-H and hold my own at the county fair each year. I love to write and read poetry, read good books, and listen to a lot of genres of music. My friends, family and writing are the most important things to me. My poetry is my best quality.

WRITING STATEMENT: The reason I write is so I can express what I'm feeling and thinking on paper instead of out loud. It helps me remember the things I love, along with the things I despise. I'm not what you call a very vocal person, so writing helps me get things out, even if it isn't loud. I don't really have a style. I just write what inspires me or what I'm feeling. It could even be a word from a song or an inanimate object on the floor. But no matter what I write about, it's all true. Everything down on paper has happened to me or I have thought it. If I wrote about things I haven't done or felt then I feel like I would be cheating myself and the readers. My poetry helps reveal a side of myself that most people won't see.

IF IT'S LOVE
SHELBY TIMMAN

If it's love, make it hurt.
That's what it's all about, right?
Make it hurt.
Cut me up and tear me into perfect pieces.
If it's love… make it hurt.
Keep me going for awhile, just so you enjoy it.
Make it hurt.

Just to leave me, all in shambles.
Since it's love…..
No protecting my heart it's supposed to hurt.
Make it hurt.
You got your wish, without saying a thing.
It's love, you make it hurt.

JACOB REHLANDER

(10TH GRADE EDISON HIGH SCHOOL; BERLIN HEIGHTS, OH)

BIOGRAPHICAL STATEMENT: I live in Berlin Heights on Rte. 113, the only octagonal house in our area that I know of. I enjoy several things: writing plays, books, poems, and of course playing and making video games. Things that are important to me are my family, my friends, my education, my poetry and literary works, my music and the feelings of others (When I notice something is on their mind, I support them.)

WRITING STATEMENT: I write to express my thoughts and feelings when I can't explain myself in speaking. I also use writing as a way to express my moods. When I am sad my poems reflect that emotion. The same with happy, angry, joyful, any emotion you can think of. You will find that when writing while re-experiencing that emotion it will communicate what you are feeling in a way that other people can understand. That's why I write, to express what my mouth can't.

I AM

JACOB REHLANDER

I am
I am the gravel
the cows the junk piles

I am the twine and wire unraveled
I am the voice that makes no sound
I am the pine cones and willows
the concrete
the steel
the blood

I am the cow skulls and smelly barrels
I am the stocker
the restaurant runner
the errand boy

I am the wagon
the puppy
the scrapie door

I am the RC car broken
the lost record
the golf balls in the pipe

I am the smoke from the birthday candles
I am the hallway kids run down
the tadpoles in the tank
the smiley face on the wall
the milk spilled

I am the no homework
the sleep in
the schoolwork on the floor

I am the ramp to the moving truck
the new room
the tire swing
the storm door

I am the new halls the new walls the
concrete
the bricks
I am

MANDY FEURSTEIN

(12TH GRADE GRADUATE PERKINS HIGH SCHOOL; MONROEVILLE, OH)

BIOGRAPHICAL STATEMENT: I live on the outskirts of Monroeville, where I spend most of my free time writing or creating art. The most important thing to me is always learning something new.

WRITING STATEMENT: I write because I have to. Something inside me just needs to get onto the paper. It's my means of communication. Writing is the best way to express myself.

CONFORMITY

MANDY FEUERSTEIN

Strip me down to what you think I am,
A doll of stuffing and string.
Assign me my position in this world.
So I'm nothing like I seem.
Cover my face with a mask
Dye my hair red, blue, or green.

Worship a book of sacred words,
Can you tell me what they mean?
Turn me into a fairy tale.
Simply take away my dreams.
Deny me of all affection,
Make me robotically clean.
Purge me of myself,
So I become part of the team.

ALEXIS E. J. LINDWAY

(12ᵀᴴ GRADE; AMHERST STEELE SCHOOL, LORAIN, OH)

BIOGRAPHICAL STATEMENT: I live in Lorain, Ohio, and participate in as many band activities as I can. I love to play my trumpet and be around my friends through band. I love to entertain and make others feel good, so being able to do that through band and writing makes me truly happy.

WRITING STATEMENT: I write because it is the most powerful way of expressing myself. I find it very easy to just sit down and express feelings so that it helps to relax me. Writing has helped me deal with many obstacles in my life when I could not talk about them. It is also something I have done since I was little and have adopted it as second nature.

BILL

ALEXIS LINDWAY

Lone little Bill
Was given a chill,
When asked of his future career.
Not much attention
Goes towards your profession,
When you've just turned ten this year.

He shivered and shook,
Scared like a crook
Who lacks a strong alibi.
Yet the motive was plain,
All he wanted to gain,
Was someone to sit and swing by.

He wanted to play,
To run and to stray
And explore and wonder and dream.
But all the adults,
Said these were his faults,
And their patience was torn at the seam.

"Be lawyer or clerk,
But don't be a jerk,
Because soon you'll be needing a wife.
Banks or nutrition,
Doctor or beautician,
It's time to figure out your life."

Bill knew in his head,
Any word he had said,
Would all have been spoken in vain.
So he ended his fun,
His playtime was done.
All his pure youth now had a stain.

He focused his time,
On becoming a mime,
Of what all the adults had to say.
His future now present,
His life somewhat pleasant.
Bill graduated today.

Bill knew they had cared,
That's why they had shared,
Their hopes for him to live well.
He took up a stand,
Diploma in hand.
Off to college to study and dwell.

Soon to a job,
Where he met Bob,
Who had suffered the same misery.
Mary and Sue,
Had gone through it, too.
With the rest of the whole faculty.

They laughed and joked,
Their faces were soaked.
Tears of both joy and pain.
Each had his story.
Of past adults with worry.
All of them too had a stain.

Time went on,
And soon Bill met Don,
And dated his sister named Terri.
He stuck with the plan,
And as a single man,
This woman he decided to marry.

Their lawn was kept,
Their home was swept
And they bought a brand new car.
Income was strong,
They were getting along,
They were told they would get this far.

Bill then knew,
That he must, too,
Share this accepted way.
He believed this was
True because
Bill's son was born today.

ASHLEY V. HARBERT

(11ᵀᴴ GRADE VERMILION HIGH SCHOOL; VERMILION, OH)

BIOGRAPHICAL STATEMENT: I live in a fairly small town right off of Lake Erie with my mom, step-dad, brother and sister. I have 3 dogs and 2 cats, but wish I had more. I don't do anything too extraordinary. I go to school, get okay grades, babysit my siblings, listen to music watch tv and play around with my computer. I hang out with my friends wherever I get a chance. I have a hard time making my mind up about anything and I show it in my taste in music. I listen to so many types, depending on my mood and the moment. And my moods change constantly. I obsess about things. I guess that's one of my faults—I think too much, sometimes. Though there are also times when I don't think enough. I guess I'm a pretty normal person with my weird moments.

WRITING STATEMENT: I remember the first day I started writing…I was just sitting in study hall my freshman year, bored out of my mind, doodling on a sheet of paper. Out of nowhere words just sort of oozed out of my pen, and they wouldn't stop. When I finished I showed it to my writer friend and she told me it was really good. I believe she influenced my writing just by being supportive of me. Ever since then I write all the time, when I'm happy, when I'm sad, when I'm confused—it doesn't matter what emotion I have at the moment, somehow I can project it onto paper. My first drafts aren't always the best, but after a little work I have something to be proud to show someone. And though I am a little protective of my poems, I have learned to take constructive criticism and put it to good use. I believe that even if I didn't show them to anyone I would still write just because it's kind of my way to cope with things. It's kind of like talking to a person only more creative. I recommend it to anyone and everyone.

PRISON IN HELL
ASHLEY V. HARBERT

Intoxicating eyes
Hypnotising smile
I break in two

Deep in the heart of your sins
The real you
I break in two

Can't walk away
Chained to you
I break in two

REPEAT
ASHLEY V. HARBERT

Together forever
Liar

The one
Liar Liar

Made for each other
Liar Liar Liar

Love you more
Liar Liar Liar Liar

Come with me
Liar Liar Liar Liar Liar

So sorry, never again
Liar Liar Liar Liar Liar Liar

Never leaving
Liar Liar Liar Liar Liar Liar Liar

Going to marry you
Liar Liar Liar Liar Liar Liar Liar Liar

ALLYSON BELMONT

(12TH GRADE GRADUATE; EDISON HIGH SCHOOL; HURON, OH)

BIOGRAPHICAL STATEMENT: I live in Huron where I enjoy swimming at my cottage. I like doing things with my friends as well—going to gymnastics, going out to dinner, and just hanging out. The things that matter to me are having the simple things that some people take for granted. Having great friends who are always there for me is very important.

TRUE FEELINGS

ALLYSON BELMONT

You wanted to say, "I love you,"
Because you thought it would last.
But I was always skeptical,
Because of things from my past.

You were there for me and you were my shoulder to cry on
Now when I'm hurt, it hurts more since you're gone.
Memories we shared were some of the best,
Especially at night, resting my head on your chest—
Not doing anything but thinking of you.
For it felt as though you were too good to be true.
You knew my secrets, along with my fears,
But leaving you is what brought me to tears.

Now we've both gone on our separate ways.
We call each other but have nothing to say.
In my mind I know what we had was true,
And I wish I would have said, "I love you."

© Larry Smith, 2006

THE MAN WHO FELL THROUGH THE SKY

MIKE HAMPTON

At a house that overlooks the biggest amusement park in the Midwest, Henry sits on the roof of his garage half-naked. His hands cradle his belly like a basketball. When he moves one palm up, the fat in his gut settles to the side without a sound. The gym shorts he wears are tighter than they have ever been before and gnaw purple lines into his pale doughboy hips. He moves his other palm up and fat settles heavy in his midsection. He lets his belly fall where it will and leans back on his arms, stretching the bubble of himself out toward the horizon. The fireworks are about to begin.

An iron structure that was meant to replicate the Eiffel Tower, but instead looks more like a birdcage on stilts, peeps over the tree line that separates Henry's home from the Great Midwest amusement park. It looms black in the night, its signal lights shutting off one by one. This is the countdown. The lights on the needle go off then the lights on the observation deck dim. For a moment the sky is blank and slate-colored, explosions are wound and waiting. Henry exhales long and curls his toes on the roof.

Rockets explode into the night, bursting out in shades of mouthwash green and peppermint reds. Paint-set primary colors streak through the air, showering sparks down onto cars hustling out of the Great Midwest parking lot below. Ten minutes pass. Chrysanthemum blossoms are born out in shimmering gold. Streamers howl in great smoke plumes, but Henry can't manage a smile. He can only watch.

When Henry was a child he loved the fireworks show. He would ride his bike down to the river to watch cinders drop into the stream every summer night before Labor Day. Now that he is middle-aged, divorced and employed by that same amusement park, the lights don't mean anything at all. Some nights like this he makes an effort to feel the way he used to, but the magic never returns.

The last barrage of explosions illuminates the spines of roller coasters spiraling around the park. The iron arms of new machines made to swing helpless visitors into the clouds reflect the firestorm above them. Henry has never allowed himself to be buckled to their flying wheels or barred into their cars. He saw a man fly free from The Mangler at age seven and in his dreams he can still see him floating free in the clouds, howling, never hitting the earth below. Each time the nightmare plays out he shudders in his sleep, afraid the man might land at his feet at last.

Positioning himself back through his bedroom window carefully, Henry looks over a poem he has been writing for his wife whom he has never seen. Her name is Rose. She is thirty-two, a single mother of two and a natural blonde. The picture Henry received from the Russian agency makes her looks silly. Her hair is teased high, her clothes are too tight and she is wearing so much make-up that it makes her look like a child who has just discovered lipstick. It's a glamour-shot kind of picture. Her head is tilted and her hand is pressed thoughtfully to her chin. The poem he is working on only has one line.

BEND ME LIKE WIRE WINGS

Henry stares at the line in his notebook. He wants to say something about roses in honor of his wife or wife-to-be. He isn't sure how these things work in Russian. He is only sure that he has to change.

To Rose he has written a great many untruths. He couldn't resist writing down all the things he wished for himself; that he is younger, better looking and has never been married. The only comfort he gathers comes from his belief that Rose must have embellished as well. She can't be as educated as she says. She must be older. *Rose* doesn't sound Russian at all. Two thousand dollars into the process now he can't turn back. It is good therapy, and a reason to change. The agency says once the paperwork is finished she could be on a plane any day, but for now he is glad that he has time and afraid of the time he has.

*　　*　　*

The next morning, Henry goes to work at the amusement park in a blue polo shirt with the Great Midwest logo embroidered on the chest. It is stained with grease and bleach, but his requests for a new one have fallen on deaf ears. His manager, who is younger than Henry by twenty years, reminds him that he will have to buy a new shirt if he is unhappy with the one he has. He has stopped asking and accepted the fact that he looks like a slob.

The roller coasters' steel girders and rails loom above the trees. Their velocity goes unchecked. The chain-pulled cars undergo maintenance only once a season at best. There are things Henry knows about Great Midwest that he does not share. He never mentions the person thrown from the The Mangler or the electrical problems that plagued The Ball Python when it was still in operation. He only keeps his distance from the rides that would kill him if they had the chance. Bodies like his weren't made to test the patience of gravity.

Parking by the R.V. lot affords Henry the only chance for exercise he will get for the next eight hours. It is a good five hundred yards to the park's main gate and the walk gets harder every day. By the time he reaches the gate his armpits have sweated oil slicks under each sleeve. He pushes his key card into the machine to clock in and waddles under the weight of the sun to the booth where he will stand flat-footed until lunchtime. Above him a sign reads "Deep Fried Oreos."

Within the hour, batter is caked on Henry's hands so thick that they become something like a welder's gloves. He can reach into the fryer and pull out a deep fried Oreo without using tongs. When he has the crusted double-stuffed cookie between his clodded fingers, he hands it to a child in line. The child's mother looks shocked, but not upset. Her face goes into the expression of someone just witnessing a bit of unexpected street magic and Henry knows that inside she believes there are things fat men know about Oreos that the rest of the world will never understand.

By lunchtime, his relief has come. An acne-scarred teenager with surfer hair pulls up khaki shorts that are falling off his hips. Henry has eaten five deep-fried Oreos by this time and has no appetite. He uses his lunch break to toddle around the park and get the blood flowing back into his feet.

Henry has brought his poem with him, or the one line that constitutes the poem, and in his crusty palms it looks like trash. In his back pocket the line has steamed to pulp and he understand that this is the life of all true poets, droning through worthless jobs with good lines turning into lint. While the clock counts down the minutes of his free time, Henry takes an ink pen out of his pocket and writes down a new line.

Burn Me Like Rose Blossoms

Back at his booth, Henry empties the deep fryers into a rolling metal cart, one by one. The oil smells like candy canes soaked in lighter fluid. Henry's polo shirt is heavy with body odor and grease but there is nothing to be done about it. He makes his way to the office to plead his case. If he doesn't get a transfer there is no hope of becoming the man he wrote he was. Behind him a young girl pins a new sign to the booth while her friend pours in fresh cooking oil. The sign reads "Deep Fried Snicker Bars."

Inside the park office, Henry's manager is trying to remember the Spanish words for "clean" and "bathroom" so he can get the new maintenance crew members to work. He thinks the word for clean is "levante," and uses "banjo" for bathroom. The confused day-workers confer with each other then scatter out the door in search of banjos that need to be lifted. Henry washes the dough from his hands in the water fountain while no one is paying attention and tucks in his shirt. His case takes shape in his mind.

Henry's supervisor explains that he will have to put a bid in for a transfer. This is the peak season after all and there aren't many slots left that meet his qualifications. Henry warns that he feels the onset of carpal tunnel syndrome building in his hands, that his arms are showing eczema and that the worker's comp settlement could grow larger with each cookie he fries. His supervisor agrees to transfer him to the water park for the time being, but warns him against false claims. There are penalties to consider, both state and federal.

Henry walks to his car free from the danger of deep fried cookies and sure of the fact that at least chlorine-resistant bacteria are, at the very least, low-calorie.

There is a letter for Henry from Russia when he arrives home. He finds it underneath an advertisement for a real-estate agency that buys homes, super-saver coupon fliers and a brand new credit card ready for activation. He takes his mail with him into the basement of his home and disrobes, throwing his clothes in the washer. He sits on an unused weight bench as he reads the letter. Promises of love follow soft pleads for patience. The paper work is moving smoothly but more money is needed.

Inside the envelope is a new picture of Rose. She wears a swimsuit and stands on a shoreline of boulders and stones. She is beautiful, but frowns as if the camera was an intrusion into some private instance in her life. Underneath the picture are instructions for electronically transferring another five hundred dollars to the Tatiana Matrimonial Service. The transfer number has changed again. Only the mailing address remains the same.

Henry pays the new matrimonial fee on his latest credit card. He plans to pay his mortgage on this card as well. The more he spends on credit, the more he has to spend. He thinks of paying his credit cards off the way he thinks of retirement and death. It is a day that will come and find him completely unprepared, but one he can't appreciate.

In his bedroom Henry watches television ads for diet pills and home weight sets. He watches hypnotists hawk tapes for weight loss and expound about the mental obstacles posed by years of dietary cruelty. Fitness is a state of mind, like loving yourself, they argue. The answer lies within.

Candy-bellied and restless, Henry can't sleep. He decides to make a plan. He will write down all the facts as he sees them. This is how daytime talk-show hosts approach life's problems in the reruns he sees. At his computer he begins to type.

When he finishes listing his woes and ambitions, it strikes Henry that this is not a plan at all, but a simple statement of facts. Change requires steps and action. He does push-ups on the floor and gets to fifteen, then does sit-ups until he gets to eight. This is a start and he rests on that knowledge.

Back in his bed, Henry sweats softly as the man is thrown from the roller coaster again and sails through the air, his body closer than in memory, shadowing the ground. Henry startles awake then rests glad that tomorrow he will be working safely away from the rides, in wading pools filled with screaming children.

*   *   *

The water park of Great Midwest is decorated with concrete alligators bleached by chlorine and the sun. They look like the boulders in Rose's picture. As Henry walks into the water park he wonders what she would look like if she straddled one of them instead. Would she look so sad? Plastic parrots are bolted to trees concealing speakers that blare golden oldies over the sunburned throng. Middle-aged women sit in deck chairs reading romance novels that rest on their bellies, while their overweight husbands toss beach balls back and forth with children on summer break.

Henry stands in his swim trunks and grins at the flat-footed parade of bodies that belong behind the wheels of delivery trucks or record desks. The young ones are tanned and glisten, but the old ones like himself all look the same: pale, frustrated, slumped with guts. He realizes that if a man wants to feel better about his body, all he need do is visit a water park.

At the water park section's office, Henry is assigned a whistle and given a new shirt. The shirt is a tank top that has a picture of a dog riding a surfboard on it. The dog is wearing sunglasses and has its tongue hanging out to catch the surf. In the mirror Henry studies himself and makes a note to mention to Rose that he has taken up surfing.

Henry's duties at the water park are simple. He is in charge of safety enforcement. This means that he spends most of his day walking from pool to pool, reminding children not to run on the wet pavement and asking people that they not remove the park's floats from the lazy river. When not roaming in search of racing children, he is to keep an eye out for unattended bags that could be snatched up by criminals, and take them to the lost-and-found department on the far side of the park. He counts up the miles he will travel in his mind and feels his stomach contracting already.

By midday the sun is unbearable and Henry searches for a shady spot to rest. His ankles swell as he wanders to the only row of trees in the water park. Vacationers on beach towels have crammed under every inch of shade.

Henry walks on, worried that he could suffer a heat-stroke at any moment, until he finds an unattended life-guard tower that overlooks a giant wave pool. For a moment he closes his eyes and listens to the sound of water being churned by children, wave generators rumbling under the ground. Russian beaches must sound nothing like this. He pictures them quiet and solemn, rocky shores with sad-faced girls placed there for American dollars. Another line comes to his mind.

I'VE FELT THE STONES AT YOUR FEET

So at peace in the lifeguard stand and in thought, Henry falls asleep. He awakens only after being shaken by another man his age who suggests Henry has his seat. The man is muscular and trim, though his chest hair has turned the color of ash. Henry apologizes and walks away confused. How does he do it? How does that man look so good at his age? It is a question Henry vows to answer.

At home that night, Henry adds the line that came to him before he fell asleep by the wave pool to the others he has collected. He knows that three lines don't make a poem but might constitute a stanza. A stanza is a good step, and when the lines come together on his computer screen he prints them out and walks around repeating them over and over to himself. He hopes that Rose speaks English, or at the very least can read English. It is a question he has never asked and suddenly he is filled with fear that all his heartfelt hopes and lies might have been left in the hands of a translator, someone less concerned with the meaning of his love letters than himself.

He sits down and types an email to the Tatiana Matrimonial Agency demanding to know whether or not Rose is proficient in English.

After reciting his stanza to himself until the words break apart into disjointed sounds, Henry turns on the television for company. He watches infomercials where the formally fat walk around exercise rigs in skimpy bikinis. The voice-over announcers ask questions while women pull on weighted cords so that their shoulder muscles pop out. Can you believe this woman is a grandmother, they ask. This can be you, they say.

Henry wonders if the man at the water park has ever been featured in any of these ads. He wonders if his basement at home is packed with exercise machines named after jungle cats that feature the signatures of fitness models. If that is the secret, Henry vows to use his credit to buy whatever he is told. If the lifeguard's body has never been strapped into padded benches with levers and bars, he must have found a better way. Whatever he is doing, Henry vows to do the same. Russian translators might have exaggerated his letters. There are untold images in Rose's mind which he must live up to.

Henry does sit-ups until he gets to twenty then goes to bed. Against his pillow, he can hear the rumbling of cars flying free from their tracks. Exhausted, he sleeps heavily and no body flies free before he wakes.

*   *   *

Henry arrives early at the water park the next day determined to find the lifeguard. While he stacks floats by the lazy river with his eyes peeled for him, the park begins to fill quickly. Mothers hurry with children to the deck chairs surrounding the pool so that they can claim the best location with beach towels before other visitors arrive. Children run to forts fitted with water cannons and sprinklers, laughing at the exhilarating experience of being blasted with cold water. Henry wonders if Rose's children are young enough to laugh at water. He has never asked their age or anything else about them, and feels swiftly self-centered. Boogie boards with the Great Midwest logo emblazoned on fall onto generated waves, but the older lifeguard is nowhere in sight. The only lifeguards around the wave pool are young and bored high school kids working on their tan for minimum wage.

The parrots are playing songs by the Beach Boys, Jan and Dean, and The Kinks. They play "Surfing Safari" then follow up with "Tin Soldier Man," which sounds to Henry like "Tense Older Man," so that is what he sings along.

As the afternoon passes Henry has given up on finding the lifeguard his age, and settles down on a bench underneath the picnic shed for lunch. He has a salad. Things in life are like poetry; small actions building towards the whole. His trunks no longer carve welts into his hips.

Just as Henry finishes the last of his lunch, he sees the older lifeguard climbing into a stand by the wave pool. As he lifts himself up onto the stand, the muscles in his back bulge out for a second, before settling into his tanned skin. Henry wipes his hands on his surfing dog tank top and makes his way casually toward the lifeguard.

Once he gets to the stand where the lifeguard leisurely watches children fake drowning one another, Henry apologizes for sleeping on the job the day before. The lifeguard, whose name is Jameson, tells him not to worry, that he does the same thing most days. Sunglasses, he says, are the key. The darker the better. They share a laugh.

In the wave pool one child floats face down with his arms spread-eagled. His friends laugh and wave their arms toward the two men standing at the lifeguard stand. Henry starts to take off his sandals and whistle, but Jameson waves him off and shrugs. The facedown boy looks up at the two with a frown before swimming off with his friends. Jameson says children are fascinated with death because they don't know what it means.

Once the drowning game has lost its appeal, children busy themselves with cannonballs and flinging one another off the side of the pool into the waves. Jameson's face draws into a knot and his hands grip the side of the stand so tight that little white crescent moons appear on his fingertips. Henry asks him how he stays in such good shape at his age, but Jameson offers no response.

Jameson rips off his sunglasses. He walks on shaking legs to the end of the pool and yells at the boys in front of their startled mothers. Henry can only make out the word "concussion" over the sound of splashing and laughter. When Jameson comes back he fishes a plastic soda bottle out of his bag. Henry asks what kind of soda Jameson is drinking to make small talk. Jameson says vodka.

Again, Henry asks Jameson how he stays so fit at his age. He confesses about his battle to lose weight and the trouble with diet pills. He asks about the newest exercise machines featured on late night television, but again Jameson waves him off. Jameson has never worked out a day in his life.

Henry tells him he is lucky to be one of the blessed few that can stay fit no matter what they eat. Jameson won't hear any of it. He argues that he isn't a genetic ideal, and says he used to weigh a hundred pounds more than he does now before at his last job. Henry asks how this is possible and after another drink from his soda bottle Jameson confesses his secret to weight loss.

According to the lifeguard, his secret for staying fit was pure unadulterated fear. He was hired as a lifeguard because he was a once commercial diver. What the park

was unaware of was the fact that he stopped diving because he almost drowned in a water tower and his nerves got to him. Now the idea of swimming locks his legs and arms. So each day he sits with the thought of someone's son or daughter taking in water in front of him. It fills him with so much anxiety that his body reacts by shedding pounds faster than he can buy new clothes. Children launch themselves headfirst into the waves. His heart rate doubles. He tells Henry that every day he works he wants to quit before something terrible happens, but the thought of becoming a slouch again keeps him from giving up. Fear keeps you fit. There are no heavyweights on death row.

Henry doesn't argue. He longs to hear from Rose and considers the prospect of terrifying himself into a dreamboat.

FEAR FOR YOU HAS MADE ME
The line starts a new stanza, as Henry takes his poem out of his glove box to scrawl it down. The roller coasters stare back at him over the trees as he drives off towards home.

On the roof of his garage, Henry watches the fireworks coming from the park. He imagines Rose sitting next to him on a blanket with her children. They watch the sparks splinter overhead and Henry promises to take the children swimming every day he works. He longs for them. He has spent his entire life on the outskirts of a celebration, and it seems a poverty to him that he hasn't shared such joy.

*   *   *

The Mangler was once the largest wooden roller coaster in the United States. It was one of the last megacoasters built before steel tubes replaced solid oak frames bolted into concrete pillars. There are no tricks to The Mangler. It doesn't spiral in loops or invite its riders to enjoy the novelty of riding while standing up or with their feet dangling. It simply offers a series of drops so profound that people with heart conditions, those who are or might be pregnant, or have any history of back problems, are forbidden to ride it. The gravitational force the ride produces is equivalent to those an astronaut faces upon re-entry. Though it has taken lives in the past, two over four decades, and been the cause of several lawsuits, it remains in operation at Great Midwest as The Mangler is still the park's biggest draw. Lines to ride it are often over three hours long. At the tail end of the line this day Henry waits in a cold sweat.

Coming to the Great Midwest on his day off is a first for Henry. He has eaten enough deep-fried, over-cheesed, batter-dipped, jumbo-sized food in his life that he has removed the mirror in his bathroom so that he never has to see his body. The park is always incredibly crowded, and Henry finds himself unable to walk through it without bumping into strangers who stare at him in disgust. It gives him an awful shopping-mall-at-Christmas-time feeling, so he stays away when his presence is not required. This day however, he has come with a purpose—transformation.

The line for The Mangler reminds Henry of the deep-fried Oreo stand where he used to work. The air itself feels vaguely oily. People sweat all around him in the maze of rails that lead visitors up to the platform where the cars depart. The scent of bodies in the heat and sticky food squirms underneath his nose. For almost an hour he takes baby steps forward, careful not to let his stomach graze the people in line ahead of him or to touch the rails which have guided millions of dirty hands up towards the machine.

In high school Henry was a member of the Future Farmers of America. At home in his basement he still has the blue corduroy jacket with his name and state embroidered on the back, although the owl and plow patch on the front is missing. While a member of the club Henry had to watch educational films about what happens to cattle at a slaughterhouse and the images come back to him now. Tired-eyed beasts taking measured steps, their bodies brushing against the processing plant's railing as they move upwards, always upwards, and disappear forever. His mouth goes dry.

Henry has cleared the first maze and made it up a flight of stairs to the second. Like the coaster, the maze of rails and stairs is made of solid oak. People have carved their names in the posts over the years and encircled them with hearts. There are inkpen markings that look like skulls and flowers, phone numbers long since disconnected are dug into the wood. Henry looks for poetry to steal. He hopes that someone in the past had only one good line in them, and that they left it written in the oak maze with hopes that another human being would understand. Nothing stands out.

There is a sound like a storm brewing above Henry, a rumbling in the sky. The sun shines bright above but the rumble goes on. Suddenly a cloudburst of terrified and joyful screams fall down as The Mangler sends thirty people in fifteen cars towards the ground at speeds their bodies would never face walking the earth. This rhythm of rumbles and screams goes over and over until Henry can't think at all. He is simply moving with the herd around him. He cannot see the roller coaster. He is inside its body. His high school teacher once told his FFA class that the cows never see the hooks and knives ahead of them, and now Henry believes him. He can only see backs and heads in shafts of sunlight, penned in, moving ever-upwards.

There is no escape. Henry is not built to glide through crowds or walk on rails. He shuffles and looks for emergency staircases that lead back to the park, but finds none. He only has time to be afraid of what he draws closer to with every shower of elation and terror above.

After two and a half hours of waiting, Henry is too weak to walk. His blood moves through his veins like buttermilk. He can see the cars now. Young children and couples step into them. The roller coaster operators look bored, high school children in charge of so many lives. He knows they never check the chains. He knows they show up late and mark off their safety checklists without inspecting anything. He knows this all without asking. They haven't learned about death either.

A girl in a blue Great Midwest polo shirt asks him to get into a car at the end of the roller coaster. It is the one he is standing in front of while he watches another girl walk down the line tugging absently on safety bars. Henry wants to tell her that he can't ride the roller coaster. He wants to tell her about the man who fell from the sky and didn't land. He wants to run away. She takes his arm and leads him into the car. She lowers the bar and raises her thumb toward the control tower. The chains pop to attention and the cars start off with a jerk before Henry can find the words.

Henry's mind feels like a beehive as he watches Great Midwest spread out beneath him. He can't answer simple questions now. He can't remember his name or what he had for lunch. He can only watch the sky grow before him and hear the sounds of chains dragging underneath his seat. They pop like splitting lumber. At the top of the first huge drop, Henry's mind clears and he searches the horizon. He sees the amusement park and the stream by his home. He sees the wave pools and the Viking ship. The Mangler has him now. It jerks with the cars in front of him down towards the earth.

Henry is weightless. He is perfectly clear in mind and spirit for a split second before his body goes through a force not unlike being pulled from an airplane at altitude.

The world goes black. Everything around Henry moves forwards and backwards at the same time. Night and day pass and return every second. He falls through the sky for two minutes but never lands. He is safe now. The chains have brought him back to the world. When the girl who escorted him to his seat lifts his safety bar, he looks at her. Still he has no words. None exist.

There are times in this world when people are blessed with the ability to step outside their bodies for brief moments and take in the beauty and disaster of their life. Some people have this ability all the time. They are given titles like shaman, life-coach or psychic. For most people this chance only comes once. It happens during car crashes, war, open-heart surgery, drug overdoses or births. Henry fell through the sky.

Henry walks to the main office of Great Midwest and quits his job. Then he goes home where he informs the Tantiana Matrimonial Agency via email that he will be arriving within the week to pick up his wife and children whether the paperwork is finished or not. He books plane tickets online, one to Russia, four back to the United States. He takes a flier from his desk and within an hour sells his home for half its value. He takes a shower and thinks about days to come when he will live in a cramped apartment with no credit. He dreams of promising a summer trip to Great Midwest to his new family who will be thrilled at the prospect of concrete alligators and gravy smothered French fries.

Henry no longer believes in steps, only blind dives into the unknown. ◆▪◆

RAIN BEGAN HITTING THE WINDOW
CAROL SMALLWOOD

We shall not cease from exploration, and the end of all our exploring will be to arrive where we started and know the place for the first time. T.S. Eliot

Rain began hitting the window: when found I'd be
    clean, rain would keep me company. I saw the
    white pine witth roots arching from its needle
    bed—to die beneath evergreen arms would be
    good.

Pillowed on runaway roots, I'd offer myself freely
    to summer rain; hear ice cracking on the lake
    heralding the close of winter; in spring I'd
    have no need to climb Grandfather's trees to
    see; in fall, leaves would round me "with a
    sleep."

No longer invisible, what wonders wouldn't I see?
    The lake, formed only 10,000 years ago, has
    molten rock just underneath.

To become part of the soil would make more sense
    than stuffed in a coffin where Aunt Hester
    would see I'd be Sunday clothes murmuring
    through thin lips, "Jesus, Mary, and Joseph!"
    while Uncle Walt would poke someone saying, "I
    got a wife who'd bleach the hell out of the
    robes of God Almighty."

WREN ON EARTH
DALE M. KUSHNER

How difficult it is to remember
the cunning I once felt
in the roar of my youth,
when the wind was my servant
and the Great Round
of shadow and light
kept its vigil with death,
but not for me.

No, not humble in those days,
thinking it would last forever,
unwilling to be restrained,
blithe at the first daggers of frost
the dense shade of my willow
growing thinner
in the thinning light,
the summer-hued hills
already converted
to the dusty tones of earth.

With a vengeance I sang
against it,
sublimely pitting mysef against the gods,
absurd in my denial of cold heaven,
never once questioning the exuberance
of faltering stars.

Lashes of rain wreck the orchard.
The broken howls of thunder
are at my door. I will be nothing
in the world's memory,

my blindness
the blindness of my kind.

Sunday Mornings
Carol Hattrup

1.
Prayer recitals in a church service
sound like hospital admission papers.
Does anything else happen around here
other than sick bodies
winding down like slow clocks with creaky pendulums?

We are here as peacocks, feathers studded with dew of holy rain.
We boarded Noah's big boat before the rest of the animals.
We can be dismayed by the grating voice
of a choir director with dyed hair and nasal tones,
run over by accent and off-key dragging on of end notes
but still be Believers.

2.
I believe I am fine sitting here, wiggling in this straight-backed pew
until a woman wafts in with her hairspray and perfume. I weep,
overcome with allergy, not emotion.

3.
Later, long after the neighbor-greeting portion of the show has passed,
the preacher will see I haven't clapped my hands
and he'll perform an autopsy
to see if divine blood runs in my veins.
Dim the lights, he'll cry,
Let's circle this girl's body with candle flame,
place the leftover crumbs of Polly's cracker on her tongue.

The congregation will carry me outside into evening,
shouting Revival to far hills, to numbered stars,
believing celebration solves logistical problems
like fevers and lost puppies
and war veterans whose minds bleed on the altar,
whose bones corrode sacred.
They will bind me to the night Tree
under which savages have heaped the sacrificial sour rinds
and sing Hallelujah under a frosty moon.

4.
Some will wander back to rest in the dim sanctuary,
sinking into hushed carpet and thick mauve cushions.
They'll dream of tamed lions with soft, panting breath
while an angel of the Lord walks among them and whispers miracles.

DISAPPEARING IN MY REARVIEW MIRROR

PAUL FREIDINGER

We were the only ones
at the Monticello cemetery.
Record heat of 97 degrees.
The old pines and oaks stayed
still in our stillness as we gazed
down on my parents' stone.
Every monument around me
bore a name I knew: Tipsword,
Wilkie, Buchanan, Brighton,
Hammerschmidt, Stiverson,
Buckingham, and Muse. Every
name had a face and a voice
that moved my memory among
the familiar. I understood what

age meant and where time went
while we weren't watching,
held the line that drew them
to me and down my face. This
is what a cemetery is: a place
to forge events with a point
of view. I found that parents
finally reach a pause, when,
without their friends, it's time
to leave and join them in the ground.
I discovered there's more of me

with them beside this plot than
left in my own uncertain days.
We didn't say a word, didn't need to,
didn't force a prayer or a plea.
We strolled away, aware of the sun
and drove on into town. Every
door was closed, every window
sealed shut, air conditioners whirring
overtime. The town might have been
abandoned since I abandoned it
myself. Echoes of ghosts on the streets
as I drove through the neighborhoods,
past former homes. I murmured
to Jan, "Growing up, I thought it was big,"
web of streets, stories, disappointments.
Burned and fought to get away
from here in order to survive. Small
town, farm town, Illinois, with
humble thoughts about how to live
and everything to give. This is where

my parents stay, in time, and all their
contemporaries, alone with me and
my version of the past. Now, the ones
in the houses dream of absconding,
like I did once. I come back on scalding
days when there's nothing in the air
but the scent of dry straw. Quiet, humble
in the presence of my mom-and-dad's
small achievements. They made it here

with all their work. I came back to
remember what it was they willed me,
my accomplishments lesser on the whole.
Maybe a sense of logic about the way

things worked and how to do a job.
Because it had to be done. There's a place
like this within a place within the
boundaries of my heart, stowed away
for the long haul. I turned off Hwy. 105 to 72,

heading to my other home again. A little
lost for what I'd lost. A pause. Less
and less to say. The pines will speak for me
when I'm gone, the way they do any season.
I'll return again quieter, more a member

than a visitor, growing fully into who I am.
Small town, farm town, Illinois, disappearing
in my rearview mirror.

60S SUMMER NIGHT.

PAUL FREIDINGER

When the red Corvair shifted
from second to third and settled on 40.
When the blacktop road crawled
over fields and wove through woods.
When the twilight.
When deer appeared in the clearing,
tawny shadows against dry grass.
When starlings were buckshot,
silent and spraying the fading sky.
When the night became night
for the next forty years.
When we got lost on purpose.
When the car shuddered over
a wooden bridge.
When we cast away the past
to recover our selves.
When a heart beat like a dove
in a nest in the stillness.
When a heart was lost.
When the car climbed over a ridge.
When the first stars.
When we spied the moon.
When the earth tilted.
When we cruised forever
on the prairie's dark tongue.

© Mark Chambers, 2006

PEOPLE OF THE MIDWEST
AS OBSERVED BY LORAIN COUNTY COMMUNITY COLLEGE PHOTOGRAPHY STUDENTS

© Mark Chambers, 2006

© Brittany Graham, 2006

© Stephanie Detko, 2006

© Danielle Grodek, 2006

MY FATHER'S GARDENS
JOANNE JACOBSON

My father loved the living world and its seasons—the visible way growing things are transformed at their time. From the first moist hint of spring he started to plan, shopping for seeds from stacks of catalogs and preparing the hard ground on his weekends off. On hands and knees he returned to the beds he had been tending for a decade in his backyard, feeling in the brush for what had survived the midwestern winter and for the places where he would have to begin again. When the sun gained enough strength, he would cup new plantings in the palm of his hand and transport them one by one to the freshly opened soil behind his house. He would give each little web of dangling roots a gentle shake, sending a dusty clump of earth flying, before he inserted it into the hole that he'd dug: dirt onto dirt, life to life. With two fingers he tenderly tamped everything down. Every once in a while he would rise slowly, bracing himself with one hand on the ground, and turn a hose to drip onto his limp plants.

On a Sunday near harvest time he would drive the whole family into the countryside that hugged Chicago's western boundaries. The high, crowded fields of corn rose impenetrably on both sides of the two-lane roads that my father loved for their closeness to the life that we were passing through. Or in the autumn he would rent a little cabin for the four of us at a state park, a single room with cots and a bunk bed made up with coarse sheets and thin, scratchy wool blankets. I thrilled to the word *lodge*: the cavernous communal dining room, its exposed log walls hung with deer and moose antlers, seemed to me like time travel, back to the frontier world of the last century that I loved reading about. And I loved the breakfasts there, when I would always order buckwheat pancakes, gritty with coarsely milled grain. But my father would be eager to get us out into the forest as soon as he had finished his food. He was roused by that edgy time of year when the trees lose their leaves and the air loses its moisture; when the atmosphere is charged with change. He could hardly keep himself from rushing ahead of us on the trail. The ground was layered with fallen leaves, long turned dark and soggy: they looked like death, my father said, but once winter came they would provide the insulation from cold and ice that mammals in their burrows beneath the surface depend on to stay alive.

The final garden of his life was my father's glory. The spring had been extravagant with heat and sunlight, and the resulting profusion put my father right up, ecstatically, against wildness. That year he printed white labels and mounted them on unvarnished pine dowels throughout the yard. From the patch of patio near his back door he held forth to members of local garden clubs. The last of the irises were still blooming in June, feathery, ruffled purple parting to reveal an intense yellow and black heart. Above the low beds of petals in a multitude of colors—pansies, petunias, impatiens, dianthus—my father had planned out elegant groupings of high stalked flowers. A narrow field of tulips, blood orange with yellow margins, was planted next to cream daffodils. Rosebushes set pure white against crimson. Close to the earth at the borders and in the shady rear lay clumps of rich, shiny green groundcover and tiny flowers, each marked with its Latin name: mint *(Mentha),* myrtle *(Vinca)*; *Pachysandra* and *Hosta lancifolia.* Like the human body, the garden remained a wonder to my physician father, the workings of order and the beauty that make life; bound, forever, to one another. The light, tufted Bachelor's buttons *(Centaurea)* shifting the eye steadily upward to the cool drama of the lilies; ivy *(Hedera)* lending strength against the forces of erosion to what flowered in the air, swaying in the faintest wind.

My father had thought that he could start from scratch there, that he could build from the fresh ground upward. He had believed that he could move to a new place and cut back the high weeds in the yard, and begin again at the colorless quick. But even then he was stuck in time's rut, as surely as the ancient insects that we saw, together, in display cases at the Field Museum of Natural History—

Father in his garden.

gripped in unyielding resin. Once he had unpacked his family in his suburban house he found that the previous owners had painted every wall grey and painted every window shut. It would take months of weekends just to sand and soak down through the shades of grey and the layers of wallpaper beneath that entombed each room, to reach the original wood. Out in the trim garage that squatted on the rear boundary of his property, Illinois state license plates were mounted thick along all four walls: a different color for each year, reaching back to before his children were born, to when he himself was just a small child and this house was being built.

What could my father do, in a world where so much had preceded him, where time was already long and primitive forces still emerged from the sea? At high tide on a Florida vacation my parents napped in the easing sun, as the beach narrowed and families around us began to collect their children and their plastic shovels and buckets. When the Portugese men-of-war floated gently in, they glowed, inflated to an unreal blue. I crept close to where they lay in a shallow pool and watched the gummy threads unwind and grope, the rubbery undersides softly pulsing a deep yellow. They lurched on an incoming wave, someone shouted—"Poison!"—and I fell backwards; gulls dipped, shrieking, over me. My father woke and he ran, but it was luck that had saved his little girl. When the next wave took them, my father stood silently and watched the bright crests recede—danger riding, facelessly, the watery surface of the earth. Behind us a man, his skin burnt nearly the hue of his orange trunks, dropped bricks on the taut hulks that the jellyfish left, dead, in the sand. They popped like kids' balloons. In his wake the fragments settled invisibly among the tilted umbrellas.

     *   *   *

By the time I finished Evanston High School human beings had managed to flee their own tired, circling planet into the cushioning silence, and yet the infinite continued to drift, inevitably, beyond them. When the Apollo astronauts pulled away from the moon they knew that they had left their footprints behind them, the tread of their bulky boots ground into the dusty soil of the lunar surface. They twisted around for a last look at their long dreamed accomplishment—and saw that the American flag that they'd planted had fallen to the rocky ground. Did they look away from one another as well—cumbersome humans; fathers—as they moved on, and down, swallowing their disappointment? Far beneath them their own planet turned in the dark, its green mantle of growing things too distant and shadowed to see. And around their hurtling capsule the world hung, *tabula rasa,* airless and empty. I imagine them strapping themselves in one final time, batting away the bits of scrambled egg and pudding that clogged their capsule after days out of gravity's reach; straining through the chill windows to catch sight of signs of life. ❖●❖

© Jason Gosnell, 2006

Our Readers Write: A Sense of Community
Edited By Susanna Sharp-Schwacke

For this issue, we asked our readers to write about *community*; anything about it. This, in turn, got me to thinking about how I personally define community. A community, like a family, is something you are placed into by birth or adoption. Or, again, like family, it is also something that you can chose, by such decisions as moving, marriage, friends, expression of religious or sexual orientation, etc.

Family is something you can choose? Yes, as in a community, one can choose who one associates with, interacts with, and is around on a regular basis. Friends become family, family becomes community. If you don't like Uncle Joe, you can eliminate him from your family or personal community by simply not talking to or about him, seeing him, etc. He still exists, but he isn't part of your core existence.

However, there still exists the larger community, part of which you have lesser control over the content of, but are still a member of. This is the town, state, country, world, and universe you live in. Each of these is a separate community, yet a part of a larger community, and you are a part of each community. As each community gets larger, though, you do not get smaller. If anything, your role becomes larger; your place in the community becomes larger as each community gets larger because there are more people whom you can befriend, influence, or be a part of their own community and life.

How big of a role you play in your communities, though, is up to you. You can be the one who sits back and lets everything play out before you, or you can be a mover and shaker, one of the stars in the ensemble cast of life around you. The more you involve yourself, the larger part you play in defining your family, your community and your life.

So, as a member by choice of the writing community, I present to you the views that my peers have on *community*.

Susanna Sharp-Schwacke
Sandusky, Ohio

I just watched an old episode of "Northern Exposure," my wife's favorite TV series. It was titled "Kaddish for Uncle Manny," and dealt with Doctor Joel's wish to have a memorial service for his dead uncle. To say a kaddish you need ten other Jews, no small task for northern Alaska. It seemed impossible for Joel, till the town of Cicely went to work, and one by one rounded up a Jewish hitchhiker, a migrating oil rigger, even a Native American convert. Joel grows hopeful and less alone till, then standing in the street, he has a revelation—the kind of epiphany this series was known for. He calls off the search and gathers the citizens of Cicely for a town meeting where he rises to thank them. Then he shares his realization with them and us, that the saying of a death prayer, the sharing of grief, is really about knowing your community, "And **you** are my community," he announces, takes up the shawl, and asks them to think of someone they have loved and begins softly saying the kaddish…camera fade out.

At a recent poetry gathering at Carnegie Mellon University I read with Diane Gilliam Fisher, Jeanne Bryner, and Lolita Hernandez, working-class poets all of us. I had read with Diane, Jeanne, Laura Bentley, and Eddy Pendarvis the week before at the Appalachian Studies Association's national meeting. I told them I felt a special bond in those readings, and Diane affirmed, "There is this kinship among working-class writers." It's another form of community shared and extended to others—readers and audience.

And so, when I think of community in the Midwest I sense this same acceptance of others…a recognition of our differences coupled with an acceptance of our common bonds that remains classless, raceless, sexless, and beyond geography. I know this is an ideal, and that Americans have become less trusting overall, but I also sense this vision of community as out there and as real as our best intentions. It's a larger vision of things, but it comes down to speaking to strangers, listening and giving good directions, taking something over to the new neighbors, or just saying thanks, how are you, and so long and really meaning it. This is a part of my place sense in the Midwest, as comfortable and reassuring as home.

Larry Smith
Huron, Ohio

When I think about the community I live in, one cliché of a close-knit town comes to mind. My wife and I did not grow up here; we had no family ties to this area. We moved here in 1979 which brings in the cliché: we are newcomers, and I stress "newcomers" as opposed to outsiders. Our sons who were born here and, most significantly, attended the local school, are villagers, not newcomers.

We were accepted, served as scout leaders, attended PTO meetings, served on school board committees, did our time in the concession stands during sporting events and never felt like outsiders just new people.

This community has a way of reacting to a family's or a person's troubles. It didn't matter if the cemetery was populated with your ancestors or if you had just appeared in town last month, if you had a problem and there was something the people could do to help, they did it. Clothing for fire victims, complete home-cooked dinners delivered nightly for the family whose child was in treatment for cancer, and of course all kinds of fund raising.

But the people here are open in their greetings and their welcome. My wife and I will always be "new" to the community until we die, but we have always been members.

DANIEL MURPHY
MONROEVILLE, OHIO

I've been so disgusted with our country these past few years, so angry and embarrassed by how we behave, how we are seen by the rest of the world. Our arrogant world supremacy, our mindless consumerism, our wasteful use of the earth's resources, our silly infatuation with the famous and vacuous. And, then, just when I find myself actually thinking about leaving the United States for a country that I wouldn't be ashamed to admit was my home, something happens to remind me of who we are, what we can be.

Last week, over six inches of rain falls over night in northern Ohio, and by morning we are surrounded by the chaos of flood.

My husband gets a call from his brother before six o'clock in the morning telling him that their crew isn't meeting at the job site. They are already heading to the home of one of their fellow workers who lives in the heart of the flooded area, just feet away from the gushing Huron River. By the time they arrive at Henry's home, the neighbors are already moving their furniture to the second floor, and, after getting whatever they can out of the yard, they watch as the river rises to within inches of the front door.

In Toledo, my sister Meg, after expressing silent gratitude for the tiny wet place on their downstairs carpet, spends the day helping neighbors with five feet of water in their basements. I can picture her, in her can-do way, lugging soggy belongings, corralling children for frenzied parents, picking up Red Cross clean-up kits for everyone on her street, and, at the end of the day, delivering Subway sandwiches to the exhausted families at every home.

And from the tiny town of Wellington, Ohio, the story of 47-year-old Al "Buz" Anderson, Jr., who, in an attempt to rescue two teenage boys stranded in their Jeep in rising floodwaters, is overcome by the current of the river and drowns. The boys live, rescued by another heroic soul.

Americans are wonderful people in an emergency. They can be so energetic and helpful and astonishingly selfless.

Remember the courage that surrounded us following 9/11 and hurricane Katrina? Those photographs of the firefighters climbing the Twin Tower stairways to their deaths. Never questioning whether it was wise, they went because they thought it was their job, because they might be able to save someone. Reports of office workers in the doomed buildings carrying coworkers down to safety—or quietly staying with those they couldn't. And in New Orleans, even a five-year-old, accidentally separated from his parents and other adults, manages to keep a gaggle of toddlers together—and safe—until they are found. We love the strangers in those stories. In the midst of the confusion and sadness, their stories are a blessing to us, and we wonder if maybe we could, in similar circumstances, be capable of that greatness of spirit.

What if, after the disasters, we held onto those feelings of love for each other, if we didn't allow ourselves to be pulled into the ugliness of fear and the pointlessness of retaliation? What would our world be like today if we hadn't squandered the world's goodwill, and instead, in an unprecedented appeal to the wisdom and compassion of the global community, we had trusted the other nations to take care of us?

What could happen still, I wonder, if we acted as our best selves, if we expanded our sense of community to accept and embrace the rest of the world?

JAN YOUNG
CASTALIA, OHIO

The geese are a comfort to me. They honk, eat and poop the same way in my new yard as they did out at the Sandusky house. While this makes them the apparent enemies of Avenbury Lakes, where they are yelled at, chased by hired dogs and generally discouraged from enjoying this multi-pond playground—I smile when I see them. Part of my attraction to moving here was that this development was designed with "Prairie Landscaping" and has a federally protected "Wet Lands" area attached.

The transition between living in Erie County and returning to Lorain County after 14 years was more difficult than I thought it would be; trying to slip from my sense of place in one community to another, from my writers/artists/ musician group to an older conservative development of 55 and over.

Taking classes at Lorain County Community College in Biomechanics and Exercise for Special Populations surrounds me with yet another group of people. These are folks who seem comfortable with "jocks". As the last kid who ever got chosen for anyone's team—it's a whole new world to me. I chose to enter this world because I feel a calling to help people attain a better quality of life as they age. I feel I should have the knowledge to back it up. I want to be a functional fitness coach for seniors. I want to fit in. But all of these changes are difficult to assimilate.

My writer community seemed to have an embracing acceptance of all people—or perhaps, just the people I identified with: the peace-nic doves, the gays, the diversity of cultures and even the non traditional pagans. And now, I feel and hear the disapproval of a deeply Christian conservative community regarding all of these topics. It isn't that they aren't friendly or good people—I just don't feel I can truly be myself.

I had a bumper sticker on my car that read Child of the Goddess with some frog decals. Over the past two years here I have learned to cloak my opinions, my spiritual preference and have tried to connect with the neighbors and make friends here. This is where I live—this is where I want to work and make a difference.

I took the bumper sticker off my car. I am still struggling with balance in my life. Science vs. poetry, day-dreams vs. work, and liberal ideas vs. conservative. But when I am feeling disconnected and lost, I look out at the pond and see the geese. I feel at home.

Honk if You Understand.

YVONNE STELLA
AVON, OHIO

© Stephanie Datco, 2006

HOME THOUGHTS
WENDY JONES NAKANISHI

"We shall not cease from exploration
And the end of all our exploring
Will be to arrive where we started
And know the place for the first time."
(T.S. Eliot, "Little Gidding,"
from *The Four Quartets*)

The young clerk at the Greyhound Bus Station in Michigan City, Indiana, told my mother that only one passenger had alighted from the bus from Chicago. He described her as a German woman who had asked directions to the nearest coffee shop.

I returned to the bus station half an hour later to find my mother distractedly scanning the bus schedule posted on the wall. She had assumed that I must have missed the bus we had agreed upon and would be on the following one. The clerk noticed us and pointed in my direction. "That's her," he confided to my mother.

We laughed about the incident in the car as my mother drove us to the town where I had grown up and where she still lived: Rolling Prairie, population five hundred.

I had apologized to her for doubting her punctuality, for disappearing for a quick cup of tea, for suspecting she would be at least thirty minutes late in meeting me.

"But why did he imagine you were German?!" my mother puzzled.

"Oh, you haven't noticed because you've seen me off and on ever since I left America. But my voice, my accent, I mean, sounds strange to people here. I'm usually mistaken for English or for Irish. Somebody once thought I was Australian. I admit, however, that's the first time anyone has ever said I was German."

Drab flat fields unrolled towards a darkening horizon. Suddenly the scenery changed. At first it seemed that everything manmade was old and falling to bits; then that everything was new and ugly. A landscape of old farmhouses with peeling white paint and porch swings clustered beside windmills and dilapidated barns was succeeded by one of sprawling one-storey, ranch-style houses, each surrounded by a large expanse of mown lawn and nothing else.

Jones family home, Rolling Prairie, Indiana.

"A new housing development," my mother informed me.

"Doesn't anybody believe in planting trees any more?"

Only the tall stems of mobile phone masts interrupted the sheer horizontality of the scenery, or the mushroom shapes of satellite dishes sprouting beside most of the houses.

"What I hate most is the loss of good farm land," my mother mourned. "And it's so quiet, so dead! Where have all the birds gone? When I was a child the sky could suddenly darken with flocks of crows. Where are all the children, for that matter? I never see any playing outside these days."

"My husband hates them. Crows, I mean! They pick at the oranges and damage them."

I felt my heart sink as we pulled into the drive. Home.

"We're home, darling!" my mother informed me cheerfully.

I felt a familiar ambiguity of emotions: depression jostled with curiosity. I steeled myself and glanced up. The old house looked worse each time I revisited it. I was never able completely to suppress the memory of words uttered by a friend several years earlier. "It looks like something out of a horror film," he had joked. He had had a point. While the paintwork was still intact, the exterior looked distinctly dingy. Late autumn was never the kindest of seasons to properties owing much of their charm to an abundance of trees and bushes, but the yard was looking not only untidy but somehow barren and desolate.

"Sorry, dear," my mother said, correctly interpreting my look. "I've had to have a few more of the trees cut down: the Chinese elm at the back, the weeping willow. I just can't cope with all the yard work. I don't mind the raking. It's having to pick up after all the twigs and branches after any storm that gets me down."

I made a sympathetic murmur, but I couldn't repress my sadness. For her, each tree represented an object to be tidied up after. For me, each was a childhood friend. I had been a lonely little girl fond of lying under trees or of climbing them.

My childhood home was of a type common in the American

Midwest in the nineteenth and early twentieth-centuries. It was a large two-story dwelling with a broad porch supported by pillars at the front. There was an attic as well as a basement, so it really represented four levels of floor space. Nearly identical houses populated the center of my small town but, on its outskirts, the traditional gave way to the modern, or the vertical to the horizontal because of the postwar generation's dislike for what was perceived as the inconvenience of stairways.

I couldn't really "see" my house, I realized, as we walked up the small pathway of crumbling cement leading towards the front door. There were many versions of the house looming ahead: from my earliest childhood memories of the dwelling, to the actual building which I was about to enter.

My family had moved into the house when I was three. After contracting polio when I was two, my father had decided to enter a new town, a new job, a new life. He had been employed as a teller at the sole bank of Syracuse, a medium-sized town in northern Indiana. He was to become the manager of the bank of tiny Rolling Prairie, a branch of the Citizens' Bank of Michigan City: a "step up in the world."

Given my age, I have only indistinct memories of those earliest years spent in our new home, but I recall it as a place bursting with life. I had an elder brother and two elder sisters. Before our arrival, it had been a structure deemed sufficiently large to house two families: one upstairs and one downstairs, with a front and a back stairway accommodating the separation of the building into two separate dwellings. But the six of us moving into it in the mid-1950's filled that house, sufficiently so that one of the large bedrooms on the second floor had to be halved to make space for a second bathroom.

Our liveliness overflowed to a large yard bounded by flowering bushes and trees and filled with a great variety of trees. We played croquet on the side lawn. The front yard was reserved for games of badminton. There was a small swing set on the boundary with our neighbor's back garden. Although my father, harboring a fear of heights, had had many of the lower branches of the trees cut, fearing mishaps should we attempt to climb them, following the dauntless pattern set by my eldest sister, my other sister and I still found many of them climbable.

We were not the only inhabitants of the property. My brother had a succession of pet dogs. My sisters and I begged for cats. At one point, there was even a rabbit. There were turtles and goldfish won at county fairs.

The town was our playground. Rolling Prairie remains a community too small to merit even being mentioned on large-scale maps of the area. Forty years ago there were few cars to disrupt bicycle rides up and down deserted streets. We children were expected to be outside from morning until dark, no privation for us on glorious spring and summer days. We occupied our three

month's summer holidays with baseball games, with riotous games of tag and hide-and-seek and, after sunset, we used to trail flocks of bats that made a curious habit of swooping down certain dark alleys. Some children liked to walk down the railway tracks bordering the town and to leave empty bottles and cans which would be satisfactorily crushed by the trains. I practiced twirling a baton with several neighbor girls, entering a competition and earning a trophy and a medal.

Like most families, we only had one black and white television, featuring at most four channels. It offered little attraction for us; there was no question of our wishing to be indoors during the daytime in the summer. We explored fields and forests. Once a train crashed in the area, and on another occasion an escaped convict was reported as having been sighted locally. He provided a suitably thrilling quarry for our hunts. It was a place of small lakes. We often were taken out for long hot days of picnicking and lazing beside watery verges, plunging into tepid waters when the heat became unbearable.

In the winter my brother led us on games of fox-and-geese through the thick snow blanketing our yard. Rolling Prairie typically had enough accumulated snow to guarantee at least a week off school each year because of impassable roads, particularly to the north of the town: a thickly-forested, hilly, rural place where the roads often represented little more than dirt tracks. The main street of the town, two blocks long, was very wide. In the deep of winter, it was divided by a five or six foot high wall of snow left by the snow plows.

We built snowmen and snow forts, staged fierce snowball fights and threw ourselves spread-eagled down on spaces of untrampled whiteness, moving arms and hands above us, and legs below, to make "angels." My mother was unable to swim, but she could ice skate after a fashion, and one wonderful year the tennis court beside the high school was flooded to make a rink.

For a town of that size, Rolling Prairie was surprisingly self-sufficient, its inhabitants well-served by a wide variety of goods and services. Forty years ago it had two taverns whose deleterious influence was offset by two churches. There was a small post office and a tiny library, one grocery story and another shop featuring an old-fashioned soda fountain, a pinball machine, and booths frequented by courting couples, each with its own individual jukebox. There was a "nickel-and-dime" shop, a hardware store, a small family-run restaurant, and a barber shop. This was in the days before large out-of-town shopping complexes had driven such small local shops and enterprises to the wall.

It was also in the days before the move to consolidate local schools further eroded civic pride and a sense of community. For my first ten years as a school child in Rolling Prairie, I walked to school. Then it was decided we needed such extra amenities as a swimming pool and a larger gymnasium, and a new high school, merging ours with that of our nearest rivals, in a place called New Carlisle, was built literally in the middle of a corn field, midway between the two towns. What we gained in "improved amenities," we lost in local pride, in a sense of belonging to a particular place. Nearly all the students from both towns had to be bussed in, and it was sad that we were forced to relinquish the old enjoyable competitiveness with New Carlisle.

The Jones children.

Now, nearly none of the shops I frequented as a child exists in Rolling Prairie. There remains only the post office, the barber shop, one church, the fire station and a restaurant. One of the taverns is still there; the other burned down several years ago, with the locals murmuring darkly of arson, that the owner wanted to recoup financial losses through an insurance payout. There is no place to buy even such a simple commodity as a carton of milk, leading inevitably to the fact that everyone must drive—in the case of the inhabitants of Rolling Prairie, to a shopping complex on the outskirts of New Carlisle.

But when I was little, none of this was foreseeable or even imaginable. I felt I was inhabiting a self-contained universe whose parameters would always be the same, lasting forever, unchanged. Naturally, in a town of that size, everyone knew each other. The town's populace was an odd jumble of "personalities." What was perhaps the town's "best" house, or the only one looking at all cosmopolitan, with houseplants actually to be glimpsed in the windows and books on shelves lining the walls, was occupied by a Jewish doctor and his family, whose clinic bordered their property. The town's most notorious gossip, an unpleasant, fat woman with two chins, acted as his receptionist. An undistinguished little house nearby, always with the curtains drawn, was rumored to belong to a prostitute. There was even a haunted house, abutting the school's playing field, which we used to dare each other to approach on Halloweens. There were no fears for child safety in those days. We happily trooped off as ghosts and witches to visit as many homes as we could, returning with paper bags gratifyingly stuffed with toffee apples and chocolates and candies and homemade popcorn balls. The only perceived danger was from the gangs of teenage boys who took advantage of the occasion to "toilet-paper" trees and to soap car windows.

But only a few years after our taking up residence there, what had seemed a fairly idyllic existence began to disintegrate. The "rot" seemed to originate, to my child's perception, within my own family. My parents quarreled more and more often. My father, who had been a kind of mainstay of the community, organizing harvest festivals and fish fries and bake sales to finance town activities and improvements, left. He was a man who liked peace and privacy, comfort and tidiness, and obviously felt he could find none of these in a household filled not only with his own noisy children but with the hordes of neighborhood boys and girls we played with. He left one summer, while my mother had taken us off on a holiday to the East Coast, never to return. They divorced two years later and, soon afterwards, my father married a woman twenty years his junior, a local girl who had worked as a teller at the Rolling Prairie bank, and returned to Syracuse, where he had managed to become the president of the bank where he had once held a more lowly position. With his departure, Rolling Prairie itself seemed to collapse, renouncing any pretensions to being anything other than a loose grouping of small-minded, self-absorbed, gossiping individuals who only happened to live in proximity to each other. There had been talk of the town's being incorporated, of a prestigious industrial development being sited in the vicinity. All of this vanished, along with my father, who had ambitiously spearheaded these potential developments.

The state of our house mirrored the crumbling world of my community. My father had been a fanatically tidy individual—a legacy of years spent in the Navy but, even more, his inheritance from an overbearing mother who insisted upon a strict regime of order and obedience. We children early were taught the mantra: "A place for everything, and for everything a place." On my father's departure, my mother lapsed into a deep depression and retreated to her bedroom, scarcely appearing, it seemed, for years afterwards. Meals were perfunctory. The furniture began to disappear beneath stacks of newspapers and magazines, piles of laundry, and unwashed dishes. I felt increasingly alienated from my siblings, parents and from the wider world, retreating into a world of books. Only they, and nature, were reliable; only literature, plants and trees could be loved without fear or confusion.

What a relief it was to leave Rolling Prairie! But first I had to endure the successive departures of my elder brother and two elder sisters. Finally, it was only my mother and I who were left. It seemed we inhabited a house filled with the ghosts of the absent, with the echoes of vanished laughter. The anger I had cherished towards her and my father disappeared in that final year, when we were the only two remaining inhabitants of the house, succeeded by a kind of desperate pity.

Apart from the occasional week of holiday or visit to my mother, I was never to return to Rolling Prairie for any long-term stay, once I had gone off to university. I have now spent twenty-one years in Japan, preceded by six months' residence in Holland, one year in France, three years in England, and four years in Scotland. Has this rambling around the world represented a kind of quest for a "home" to replace the one I had lost in my childhood? Perhaps.

Oddly enough, it was when I first visited England at the age of eighteen, on a six weeks long high school package tour through Europe, that I felt I had inadvertently stumbled upon my spiritual "home." It seemed strange because the landscape of the region of England I felt—and continue to feel—most drawn to, could scarcely be more different than that in which I grew up. I was thirteen before I had my first glimpse of an ocean and fifteen before I ever saw a mountain. The area in the northwest corner of England—the Lake District and its environs—where one is never far from the sight of hills and mountain ranges sweeping down to the sea, was the place where I experienced an intense sense of homecoming, of having finally arrived at the place where I was meant to be.

I knew that this was partly attributable to my past. I had imbibed a love of reading, and particularly of English literature, from my mother and her mother, and that area of England was inseparably connected with some of my favorite poets. I had memorized Wordsworth's "Daffodils" and portions of Coleridge's "The Rime of the Ancient Mariner" in primary school. Were I an individual who believed in reincarnation, I might be inclined to believe that I must, in an earlier life, have lived in this part of the world. The grey stones composing the region's houses and its walls, the thick green hedges bounding the fields, the grazing sheep, the shrieking of the strong winds which batter the region, and the burbling of the tiny brooks and streams which crisscross a countryside of rolling green pastureland stretching up to moors and barren fells; these all feel poignantly familiar and even beloved.

Yet my first year in Britain represented a struggle. I had arranged to spend a "Junior Year Abroad" period at Lancaster University. I found the regional accent difficult to understand; I was initially unable to adjust to a diet dominated by hot tea, fish, chips and mushy peas, and salad sandwiches. I was appalled by the lack of central heating or of the unlimited supplies of hot water to which I had been accustomed as an American. I ruined many skirts in my first months in Lancaster, scorching them with my habit of huddling over electric fires.

I was also unprepared for the anti-American sentiment I encountered, expressed by English friends in affectionate teasing, and by the ill-disposed, in criticism or even contempt displayed towards my country. It proved a salutary, if often, upsetting exercise: the unsettling of previously unquestioned assumptions. I had assumed the world consisted simply of an extended, if far more cosmopolitan, version of Rolling Prairie. I was soon disabused of such innocence. To my chagrin I learned that not everyone shared my ideas about life, and I was to gradually discover how subjective and limited my perceptions were, shaped by my own experiences as a child growing up in the American Midwest in the 1950s and 1960s.

This pattern of the broadening of horizons, mental and physical, is one that has been repeated throughout my entire life. I left the tiny town of Rolling Prairie to become one of 35,000 students attending the Bloomington campus of Indiana University, naturally encountering a variety of individuals far more diverse than any I had met in my childhood and required to meet academic challenges far beyond those required by my provincial high school. The "Junior Year Abroad" spent at Lancaster University represented another opportunity to "grow"—leading to feelings of being at once exhilarated and threatened.

On graduating from university I felt I faced two paths: to enter a law school in America or to do something entirely different, for at least a year or two. I chose the latter, driven by what has always, I now realize, been the underlying determinant of my behavior: the belief that I have only one life, that it represents a wonderful, special experience, and that it is up to me to live each day in such a fashion that I will feel as few regrets as possible when I am to die, coupled with a conviction that something's promising to be "difficult" is no reason not to do it, but, rather the reverse.

Inspired by the pattern set by the elder sister of an English boyfriend, who had become an *au pair* girl in Zurich and subsequently married a Swiss surrealist artist, I decided to travel to Paris to work in a French household. I only lasted three months. The wife was a stylish young Frenchwoman, fluent in English, who had met her husband, an Air France pilot at work; she had been employed as an air hostess for the same airline. He had aristocratic connections and was kindly and indolent. She was ambitious, intelligent and shrewd. They had two small children for whose care I was supposedly hired but, given the fact that the couple employed a Portuguese maid on a daily basis and that Madame loved cooking and childcare, I was given nearly no duties.

This might sound enviable, and it was by many of the friends I made there: young British and Swedish girls who worked long hours every day, earning no more than I did, laboring away at cooking, cleaning and childcare. But it also meant that I felt lonely and bored. It seemed I had only been employed as a status symbol. I came to realize, too, that I felt simply too old to occupy such a position in any household. As an American university student I had been used to a life of independence and intellectual stimulation. As an *au pair* I was expected to obey curfews and to play the role of an obedient, if rather servile, member of a household of which I knew I never was really a part.

My feelings of frustration led me to inform Madame that I would be moving into a neighboring city with my English boyfriend, to set up an informal English language school there. He had a full-time job at a local Berlitz, and I taught French housewives, children, and businessmen. We easily "made a go of it" for the following seven or eight months, before I felt I must leave to return to the States, to earn money which would help finance a Master's degree I hoped to undertake at Lancaster University.

Of all the countries in which I have made "my home" since leaving the United States, admittedly, France felt the least like any place I could come to consider as a "home." Of course, there was the different language to contend with. The French friends I made often scolded me for spending most of my time with compatriots or with Canadian, Australian, or English friends, rightly pointing out that I was wasting a perfectly good opportunity to become fluent in French. But so much felt "alien" about the French culture to me that I was reluctant to abandon the lifeline offered by friends with whom I could feel happy, easy and secure. At the risk of making generalizations or of committing the sin of expressing social stereotypes, I must say that it seemed the French enjoyed "argumentativeness," regarding it nearly as an art form, one in which they engaged on the slightest occasions, and with great passion whether the issue was a trivial or an important one. I had heard too much of quarreling in my childhood for it to hold the slightest attraction for me, and I dreaded provoking the verbal onslaughts which seemed consonant with fluency in the French language.

It was with some relief that I returned to Britain, after a short spell spent in Chicago, working as a secretary, and in Holland, living with hippie friends in a "squat," first to earn an MA in eighteenth-century English studies at Lancaster University and then a Ph.D. in the same subject at Edinburgh University. My French friends had complained at the English "reserve." I found it reassuring and relaxing.

In my last year of working on my doctorate, I applied for a position at a small private Japanese university open only to a graduate of Edinburgh, the Japanese dean of the faculty of arts of his college being anxious to establish some link between his institution and the British university where he had spent his sabbatical year. I vividly recall my English boyfriend's reaction to the news I had applied. "Some people wouldn't know an opportunity if it bit them on the nose. Good luck! These chances perhaps only come once." Given my lack of experience, my few teaching credentials, I was surprised to have gotten the post. I later learned that discrimination had worked in my favor, that the Canadian man who was my closest rival for the job was not accepted because of fears he might prove a predatory western male.

At each point in my travels crisscrossing the globe, the temptation has been to retreat to the familiar and the secure. I am glad to say that it is an inclination which seems to be diminishing rather than increasing with my own advancing years and the experience of life, and confidence in my own abilities to cope, that they have conferred.

I imagine my childhood friends would have characterized me as a girl who was lonely and shy, who dreaded attracting attention. This was especially true in the difficult years after my parents' divorce, when I remember crossing the street, or even retracing my steps to avoid having to meet or to greet people walking in my direction. I dreaded speaking on the telephone and would pay an elder sister to carry out the simplest tasks required of me—for example, going to the grocery to buy milk—simply to be able to avoid painful human contact. My mother still marvels that the daughter she imagined would be content to live out her days in a small northern Indiana town like Rolling Prairie has ventured halfway across the world. It seems in retrospect as though each successive move I have made in my life has been one entered into in preparation for the ultimate challenge afforded by life in Japan. These early experiences toughened me physically and mentally

In Japan I found, for example, that I must suffer the privations and discomforts I first was dismayed to discover in England. For over ten years, I inhabited Japanese houses which not only lacked central heating but also flush toilets. My first home had no hot running water and was so flimsy that I imagined I could easily knock down its plywood walls with a sturdy mallet; certainly, it offered little protection against the surprisingly cold Japanese winters, and by the time the monsoon season arrived in mid-June, it seemed to have gathered within its dark, cockroach-infested confines the mercilessly hot, humid temperatures, disturbingly transforming itself from a winter freezer into a summer furnace.

My difficulties in learning French provided a foretaste of those I would encounter, and still daily experience, in living in a rural community in southern Japan in which I am one of very few native English speakers. Now, when I hear French, it sounds impossibly easy because of its easily-grasped similarities to English. Japanese, on the other hand, presents not only a completely different grammatical structure, but is a language expressed in four different writing systems, all of which need to be mastered to be able to be considered "literate" in this society.

But I think what I found most difficult was the shock of the loss of privacy. In a sense all foreigners—and especially western ones—are public property in this still largely homogeneous country. This was particularly true twenty years ago, when I first arrived in Japan. Local schoolchildren used to wait outside my home and follow me down the streets, echoing English phrases they had learned at school. I performed simple tasks like grocery shopping to the accompaniment of little boys and girls popping out in front of me to say "Harro," (Hello) and "Zis is a pen."

At first, in the initial difficult months, I thought I simply would not be able to cope. I was depressed and wept often and probably drank more beer than was good for me. Gradually I became accustomed to my new life. Of course, there have been compensations as well as privations. I particularly treasure the Japanese reluctance to invite social conflict. They must be among the most polite people on this earth, apart from the times when they are behind the wheel of a car, and human aggressiveness and selfishness are allowed free display.

Nineteen years ago I married a Japanese farmer. We and our three sons, aged seventeen, fifteen and ten, inhabit a large wooden house bounded by a high hedge and surrounded by tall trees. Visitors to our home marvel at it, invariably exclaiming that they feel they have been transported to the U.S. or to Canada when they enter the front door. It's fortunate that I married a man whose dream was to build his own log home; it means that life in Japan is never quite as "strange" or "challeng-

Nakanishi home, Japan.

ing" as it doubtless would be were we to live in such a house as his parents inhabit, with its tatami mat floors, removable paper walls, and Buddhist altar, a home decorated by calligraphy scrolls and formal flower arrangements.

The students at the university where I've been employed since my arrival in this country usually imagine that I am English. I fail to conform to the stereotype of the loud American which many of them hold. As for me, I feel terribly privileged to have been able to experience at first-hand so many cultures. I feel, too, less and less inclined to identify myself particularly with any of them, which was not always the case. I was appalled when, shortly after my arrival in Japan, an American woman I chanced to meet who had already resided in this country for some twenty years admitted she felt far more at home in Japan than she did in the States. At that time, I could scarcely imagine harboring such an attitude.

Now I find that I feel the same. Not only am I invariably taken to belong to another nationality when I visit "home," but I find that the American language and particularly its slang changes with such amazing rapidity that I need to interrogate friends and siblings about the current new trendy phrases simply to understand basic English conversation there.

I have become a foreigner in my own country. I feel the awkwardness and discomfort of a visitor in a strange land when I visit America. When shopping at an Indiana supermarket several years ago, for example, I was taken aback when the young woman at the cash register demanded my answer to the question of "paper or plastic." The thought that she might be asking whether I preferred to pay by credit card or by cash floated briefly through my mind. Finally she impatiently thrust one paper and one plastic shopping bag in front of me, indicating that that was the choice I needed to make. It is now a struggle, too, to drive in the States; Japanese drive on the other side of the road and observe different traffic rules.

In any case, in my absence, the America of my childhood seems to have altered beyond recognition. I am sorry to say that most of the changes sadden me. The little local shops which once dominated communities like Rolling Prairie have, by and large, disappeared, replaced by franchises on the outskirts of all towns, meaning that they all look somehow alike. In the name of "progress" and "convenience," small winding roads have been widened and straightened; everyone seems to live in ranch-style homes; and trees and gardens have made way for large parking lots. Too, after living for so many years now in countries which prohibit private ownership of guns, I can actually feel physically frightened at being in America, where random violence seems alarmingly commonplace.

What is "home?" The old adage holds that "home is where the heart is." I've come to believe that that definition is too limited. I now feel that we can each of us, like the turtle and the snail, carry our home with us, but for humans, the home lies within, not outside the body. If we can learn to find happiness and a confident self-sufficiency inside ourselves, allowing us to be willing to meet new people in a spirit of openness and respect, we need never consider ourselves "strangers," wherever we may be. In our new age of internationalization and globalization, we are told that we must consider ourselves "citizens of the world." In a sense, I agree with that assessment, but, just as I treasure my memories of the Rolling Prairie of my childhood, I also think we must never allow ourselves to forget the particular place and circumstances which shaped us.

My immediate family seems to represent a kind of microcosm of the circumstances we must embrace in this brave new twenty-first century. I have lived in five different countries. My husband has lived in two, spending three years in Kenya with the Japanese equivalent of the American Peace Corps. I teach English at university and he is not only self-employed as a farmer but he also works at the same institution on a part-time basis as a Swahili instructor. Our children speak mainly Japanese but can understand some English. My relatives live in America but most of my closest friends are in Britain and Japan.

Wendy Nakanishi and her family, Japan.

When my husband and I take our children abroad on summer holidays, as we try to do, finances permitting, we sometimes ask them if there is a favorite item they wish to take, thinking it might be a toy or a book we could carry with us, to minimize their feelings of discomfort or strangeness at being away on a trip. We are always amused when our sons request, as they invariably do, that we somehow manage the feat of taking our dear log house with us, telling us that it is what they miss most when we are away. I think we all find ours a particularly "home-like" home: a refuge, a retreat, a place of comfort and happiness and laughter. It is a Japanese custom, when returning to one's house, to say "tadaima," or "I'm home," whether or not anyone else is expected to be there. It is a word we are all fond of uttering.

Now, while my children still make their home with us, my husband and I consider this house in Japan as the place where we were meant to be. But we both can easily, if rather sadly, envisage the day when our three dear boys must "fly the nest," and it will devolve upon us to find our new "home"—whether it be in a place where he and I will continue to live together or take up new, separate lives, or whether it might be in Japan or America, in Africa or in Europe, or even in some place we have yet to visit. ❖❖❖

EMPTY NEST

JUDITH FORD

One gone, the other almost. Your heart aches as if
both were dead; the girl moved to Boston; not gone,
you tell yourself, two hours on a plane, you tell yourself,
for all the good it does you. In seven weeks, you will pack
the boy into the red Subaru with his Einstein
poster, his geometry sculptures, towels and sheets,
band-aids, antihistamines, melatonin, shirts and
pants, lots of clean underwear, boxes of books, Kleenex,
toothbrush, cell phone, laptop computer; while
back home, the matted stuffed dog, Arfie, guardian
of sleep, witch-repellent, loyal comforter
and witness, smelling of the boy, lies flat with grief
on a pillowless bed; in Burton-Judson Hall,
no one to share Nic's room, his midnight self-doubt,
no one there to help push back the empty dark
when late it rises up and howls.

Seven weeks and he will go, will set his shoulders, set
his gaze ahead and walk, through the iron arch of
Hull Gate while bagpipes and you weep into countless
tissues; all of it as it should be, as you wish it to be; Nic
won't see the threads fray and snap, fly free; you will feel
every one as it sings through the air coiling back on itself,
returning to you, to curl up, spent, dying, its purpose served.

When they are born, no one tells you this, the dirty secret
of parenthood, that you will lose them not just once,
but many times; one day you look for the infant and he
has vanished; you look to gather up the four-year old,
"Jessie!" you call, "time for your bedtime story," a teenager answers you with scorn; you want to pull the first-
grader onto your lap, hold him close, bury your nose in
his sweet child-smell but look, he is taller than you,
barely allows a quick hug, kiss on the cheek, even
when you can see the fine lines that shadow his skin
everywhere, how he is about to crack wide open,
you wonder if he's ready and how he
will bear it.

Can you bear it, this strange parade of children, how they
come to you at all the ages, having inserted themselves
into your every cell, rushing past, leaving ghosts: the newborn,
the new-walker, the one crying, "watch me, Mom, watch,"
as he flies out over turquoise seas, the white shadows
that cling to your knees and shoulders, you catch a glimpse
of the passing heel of the ten-year-old, stepping
around the corner; they weigh your heart, push
tears up into your eyes, you feel their small hands in
yours, the warmth of their tiny bodies curved against
your side, never in focus anymore,
always there, always gone.

Would you have taken this on if someone had told you,
"at the end, you will wake in the night, many nights,
and mourn the little ones who have not died, the times
you failed them, your own young selves, the acceleration
of time, the landslide of years gone by before you could
tuck them safe away;" would you have dared, had you
known how many times you would be sliced
clean through by these, the twin blades
of embrace and bereft?

DAD SPEECH
NUMBER NINE
EMILY BOBO

He says, daylight savings killed
the drive-in. It's early spring. Morning.
We're driving lumps out of the tires
on his rusted green Ford.

Used to be a family could go
see a show, Bambi at 8,
Rambo at 10, popcorn, hotdogs,
soda pop, beer, 10 bucks, he says.

Our progress creates friction,
holds us, beltless, to the splitting
seat, heats the rubber wheels,
rounds out edges.

Can't buy family nights
like that anymore. You want to
take them to a movie—25
bucks—no sweets, no treats, no beer.

We're driving fast now. Two
lane highway, curves, low bridges, no
cars, just tractors, trucks and
grasshoppers on the windshield.

Don't know why they want to save
the light. Seems there's enough,
he says, and slowing the truck,
turns back home.

THE BAD KID
WILLIAM DeGENARO

I recall the moment
around 1981
when you became the school's
bad kid

Bus six

I'm in first grade
you fifth

You slugged me
maybe hard
though I didn't cry
maybe just a tease
of a punch
though I don't recall
which one

I told my teacher
she told your teacher
and that was that

Now you're
Ozzy Osbourne cassettes
summer school
repeated grades
pocket knife

Also the always time
for Nerf football
games in the yard
ice forts on snowdays
a ride to the pool or the ymca

Also the gap-toothed grin
the dirty joke
the AC/DC lyrics
with a bad word

Around 1993
I recall the
dorm room
case of Bass
a contraband live
Christmas tree
Smashing Pumpkins
or maybe Pavement
on a cheap boombox
and a phone call
from home:
you, your great-aunt,
a struggle.
fifteen bucks,
a history of crack,
a murder charge,
front page

And sitting among
beer cans
new friends
philosophy textbooks
I hang up and
recall
the moment
you became
the bad kid

THE FALL OF A GILT ANGEL
LOIS BARLIANT

The angel's wings glowed from the lights at the back of the antique shop at Clark and Roscoe. Gabriella pushed the handle, and the door swung open, dragging her into the shop.

"Are you open?" Dust on vintage coats and stacks of furniture ignored her call. "Anybody here?" She tiptoed into the half-lit shop. Finally, she would see the angel up close.

A rubber mat for rain-like the downpour that morning–stretched halfway to the back counter. From the street, the bronze-gold angel appeared to have beckoned her. Gabriella knew she couldn't buy him. He probably wasn't for sale, but she wanted to see his face. Every day when she ran for the bus, she saw the golden wings spread across the back wall, but the shop closed at five and she didn't get home until seven.

A refrigerator hummed somewhere. She heard the scratch of a second hand against the face of a clock. "Hel-lo?" she called out. Nothing. Why leave the door open like that? Usually the iron grid to prevent burglaries spanned the door and windows with clamped fist-sized padlocks. The 'antique' shop had junk, but her mother had sold a stroller like the one in the window for $350. She coveted a set of 'Jellystone' juice glasses crammed on a table with odd pieces of china sets, diner mugs, and casseroles without lids. Near the glasses, stainless steel canisters from flour to coffee, cloaked in grime, appeared to be in mint condition. Somebody should be watching, or the shop would be robbed blind.

She looked up at the angel. Maybe the shopkeeper thought that piece of painted wood protected everything. Maybe it did. Perched or braced above the showcase on the back wall, the angel peered down on the counter. Grungy wires held the wings about six inches from the ceiling. Nobody had troubled to dust the brassy feathers. Bronze curls topped his head, but the tilt of his face kept his features hidden. She stared up to read the angel's thoughts. She had this notion that he was aware of her—especially if she was late.

The shop was empty—except for the junk and the angel. Chairs stacked to the ceiling on the north wall appeared to be old residents and the typewriters and adding machines wore thick coats of dust on the keys. Gabriella stepped between a table stacked with dishes and another crowded with lamps and dresser sets. Directly in front of her on the counter, she noticed a cluster of rings.

A sky blue velvet pincushion-like heart-shaped box held rings in slits so they stood straight up. Gabriella didn't want to move, blink, or breathe. She pressed her tongue against the roof of her mouth to keep from mak-

ing a sound. No dust on the sparkling gems. She wasn't supposed to be there, but she forced herself to breathe, and the muscles on the back of her neck relaxed a little.

The angel, a piece of wood carved with a face and wings, stared down, but Gabriella ignored him. She wanted to try the ring that was the same color of blue as the velvet. Fine rays of white light radiated from the center in the jewel. At first she didn't dare touch it, and then she pulled it out of the slit and put it on her right ring finger.

"May I assist you?" The man's voice came from directly behind her ear.

Gabriella hadn't heard him walk up. His breath felt like strands of dusty gauze draped her arms, jaw, back, chest, legs. Even her fingers and hair—her eyelashes felt constrained. She couldn't move.

He stepped next to her. Blond and skinny, he wore a suit from the 1940's. Not retro, old. The shiny dark brown pants sagged at the knees, and his jacket sleeves hung out of shape. Gray whiskers had escaped the razor at the back corner of his chin.

"I'm just looking," she said. The ring sparkled on her finger. "I came in to see the angel." She looked up at the gilt statue. The face looked down at her with angry eyebrows and a stern mouth, as if it didn't like her answer. She saw herself standing at the counter in loose white jeans that hung on her hips and a sun-yellow halter. "How much is the angel?"

He laughed through smoker's phlegm and looked up at the bronze face. "So you came for the angel and decided to try the rings." His eyes went from the ring on her hand to the halter she had knotted tightly to make her breasts look fuller. "You're welcome to try them all. You have lovely hands. That sapphire looks gaudy on some women." He turned and walked to the entrance.

"Just let me lock the door," he said, glancing over his shoulder in her direction. "As you may have noticed from the sign, the shop doesn't open until noon. I have a private client coming to look over the rings at eleven."

Gabriella had wanted to try other rings. And she wanted to see the necklaces and bracelets in the glass cases of the counter. One necklace had strands of diamonds hanging from the main chain. In the dim light, it seemed to collect energy and send it off, clear and independent of other light. She wondered if it would shine in the dark, but she doubted it. Hearing him turn the key and pull it out of the lock, she glanced at a door in the back that had a chain and a padlock.

"I was waiting for the bus, but I saw the light in the back, and I tried the door. The 36 should be coming now." She looked down at her hand and couldn't help admiring the ring on her finger. The sapphire made her feel privileged, rich, like someone who didn't scrounge at the office on Saturdays.

"You just missed a bus. It drove away from the stop as I locked the door. Since they don't come that often on weekends, you'll have time to try on the yellow topaz or the tourmaline." He stepped fast, silently on rubber-soled shoes, and stood behind the counter.

He didn't expect her to buy the rings. Being in the locked store with him seemed B-movie creepy, but she wasn't afraid. She could take him down and pull the key out of his pocket, if it came to that. Why not try on the rings? She slipped the topaz on the middle finger of her left hand and compared that gem with the sapphire. Her hands could have been in a *Vogue* magazine ad.

She took the rings off and fit them into the slits of the display heart. "Thanks for letting me look even though your shop is closed."

He pulled the sapphire ring from the tufted heart. "This stone will never lose its beauty. The light that comes out from the center will be there when the last trumpet sounds." He pointed up toward the angel. His eyes were old person clouded, still blue. They went from her face to her body like he was estimating the value of her bare shoulders or the part of her breasts he couldn't see under the yellow halter.

"Would you like to wear the necklace?" he asked, as if he knew which one she had singled out. She glanced at him, knowing he wouldn't miss the desire she had to hold it. She shook her head and stepped back, but he opened the case and lifted up the cluster of glittering diamonds, stars falling from his hand. Even before he came around to put it on her neck, she knew how luxurious the weight would feel against her skin. In the mirror on the wall behind the case, she saw herself—gorgeous—sparkling in the necklace. The yellow halter wasn't what she would wear with diamonds, but it was exactly right.

Behind her, he stood, and, as she watched in the mirror, he raised his hands to her chest and undid the knot of the halter. She let him. She almost wanted him to even though he was old and ugly. To him, she was beautiful. And when he pulled the halter away, she let him cup her breasts in his hands. They were calloused and the cracked skin scratched, but it made her skin feel all the more tender.

But when he leaned forward to kiss her, she pulled away, grabbed the ties of the halter, and knotted them back together.

"Don't." The force of her own voice startled her. "Get away from me." Her voice kept going, as if some part of her overpowered the fear. "Leave me alone." She turned to face him; her face burned.

She heard a noise, a crack, but loud. One of the wires that held the angel to the ceiling snapped. The other wire strained; Gabriella knew it would break. The angel would crush her and the letch. "Watch out!" She flung her body against the old man, toppling him. Dust clouds puffed in the explosion of shattering glass and splintering wood from the counter. Necklaces, bracelets, rings, pins, and confetti-colored costume jewelry scattered in every direction. Gabriella saw the angel's right wing resting an inch above her foot. He still frowned but, as far as she could tell, he had survived the fall intact.

The old man lay still.

Gabriella grabbed his shoulders and shook him. "Hey. Wake up. You're all right."

His mouth opened wide to suck in air. His eyes opened, rolled back, then stared up at the ceiling.

Gabriella glanced down at the necklace he had put around her neck, yanked it off, and threw it on the pile of debris. Shards of broken glass glistened next to precious jewels and polished stones on the floor. She moved slowly to avoid cutting herself, got up on her knees, and then stood in the rubble of the counter. She looked down at dark gray fur on the back and wings of the angel. Years of dust-laden grime covered the gilt.

The old man lay on his back where she had pushed him. His eyes were closed. Blue veins crisscrossed his thin eyelids. His face looked like gravestone marble except for speckles of red on his cheeks. She said, "Are you okay?"

Tears traced wrinkles down his temples toward his ears.

"Are you all right?" She asked again.

His mouth opened, and then closed, tight. He raised his right hand a few inches and let it fell back down to the floor. He said something too softly for Gabriella to hear.

"I'm going to call a doctor," Gabriella said and pulled her cell phone out of her pocket.

The man's eyes opened. He waved his hand "no" to get her attention. "I'm sorry," he whispered. The dust muffled his voice. He closed his eyes again. Maybe he couldn't stand to see the destruction of the store.

"The key is in my pocket." He wheezed with each breath. "Will you forgive me?"

"Give me your hand." She wasn't sure that she hadn't caused the angel to fall. "I'll help you up." It was like his fingers were still on her breasts.

He hadn't moved, but he looked at her. He held his hand out to Gabriella and she pulled until he was sitting in the shattered counter of jewelry.

Gabriella looked back at the counter and the shelves in ruin on the floor. The filthy angel lay as if hovering over his personal hoard. Gabriella gave her hand to the man sitting in front of her and helped him get to his feet.

"If you want, I'll help you pick up this stuff." Broken jewelry lay everywhere. "Thank God that angel missed us."

"Yes." His voice was flat. "We were fortunate." He rubbed his hip. "Me, especially. You pushed me out of the way." He bent over the angel, but didn't touch it.

"You don't realize how beautiful you are." He could have meant the angel or Gabriella.

He took the key from his pocket and walked to the door. He winced as if one leg had been hurt. Gabriella followed him. After he opened the door, he stood in Gabriella's way. "Forgive me." He looked at the bright sunlight in the street.

She watched the No. 36 pull away from the curb.

"Yeah," she said and stepped out into the street, but she avoided his eyes.

She thought about the diamonds. When she heard the door close, she said, "It was my fault too."

❖■❖

OJIBWE LAKE
MITCHELL METZ

Not long after evening loons, war whoops echo
between the moon and its rippling twin—

another band of drunken Illini
manifesting their destiny in my Wisconsin.

I drive here on occasion to fish, drink beer,
and become offended. Gramps drove here to fish.
Dad to fish and drink. Among my people
this passes as legacy.

I court this lady with violent silence
because her face pales when I say her name:
Ojibwe Lake. My lips kiss the syllables
like an itinerant lover, my tongue
licks her identity on the cheap.
So I squat by the fire, dumb.

The Pabst in my veins inhibits imagination
or I'd consider the posture, moral or otherwise,
of Ojibwe braves two centuries past, absently poking
the embers of their doomed heritage.

Did these indigenous wraiths, like me,
watch wan little figures strut past fires too large,
listen to whiskey shatter the surface tension of night—
and adopt the mammoth umbrage of a nation besieged?

Or merely wonder who they are
and why they're afraid of the dark?

WHAT IS TOUCHED TO REACH SOMETHING ELSE
RODNEY TORRESON

is what you become
after the Sioux Massacre:
reeds the Sioux bend aside
to view your tent.
A moccasin arches
over a leaf without touching it;
you are that leaf,

everything but yourself
standing beside mother,
as her smile welcomes
two Sioux
near our sunshade.

They present a sack
you decide to be part of
in that opening motion
of their hands.
When you learn it is
to be filled with flour,
you are the drooping mallards next
handed to her,

the hollow of the chief's quills
you add to the chided wings
of the dead.

You flap treeward
as she passes the flour
to one called Slow Feather,
his cheeks scraped like pottery—
who sees through the arrow
a splitting spleen
of an age out ahead of them,

you now ashamed,
a little emptiness
in the will of Chief Hole-in-the-Day
for a child who does not know
his own skull.

HATCHET JOB
BOYD BAUMAN

What if the waves of the prairie had been more foreboding than the sea
and the green blades cut deeply, no matter how they were parted?

Imagine Sitting Bull as more proactive
letting Crazy Horse run amuck
and push their advantage after Custer no longer stood in the way.
Chief Joseph may have been emboldened to say, "From where I stand now,
I will fight for our sovereignty forever."

Lincoln could have been forced to extend
an Emancipation Proclamation to all complexions.

Instead of terrorizing the Navaho,
Kit Carson could have been as benign as his name.
and Sheridan would have been a fringe radical with statements like,
"The only good Indians I ever saw were dead."

If buffalo had been a more elusive target
perhaps Groundhog Bill would've been a laughingstock
A moniker assumed by rodeo clowns
and all cowboys too timid to ride bareback.

I could almost imagine a childhood where
the cowboys would've been decided underdogs
even on the few concrete playgrounds.
I could've tuned in to hear the hero Tonto's elegant discourse
interrupted only by the Lone Ranger's cheesy catchphrase.

Kids would learn to play *kapucha toli* before even football
and America's team most certainly wouldn't be found in Texas.
The battles in the school board would rage:
Evolution, or did the Raven create the world?

In college, I could read about the Trail of Triumph
in the native Cherokee
and manage a spring break visit to the carvings of Chocice and Geronimo
in the hills of the Dakota Territory.

And, if my buddy had been a Euro giver
about the tickets he'd promised me
I could just get a couple from a shot gunner myself
and catch the Kansas City Presidents vs. the Washington Pinkskins
or the Cleveland Caucasians vs. the Atlanta Cowards
depending on the season.

FISH STORY
TROY TRADUP

BOOM!

The rear door of the hardware store bursts away from all three hinges at once and slams to the floor like something out of a Tex Avery cartoon. The four of us tumble inside, already soaked to the skin, and then a tentacle of wind-driven rain follows and slaps us all on the collective behind for good measure. Samuel heaves the door back into place to keep out the worst of the deluge that's raging outside, and the rest of us stand there for a moment looking dazed and more than a little stupid. Steam rises from our shoulders like wisps of better judgment.

Father Mike is first to shake off the effects of our disorienting entrance. "Jesus H. Christ!" he bellows.

This energizes Miranda. "Are we *trying* to wake the sheriff?"

The squeaky finger of blame begins to make the rounds—once, twice, half again a third time—until the crackling adolescent voice of our leader, the aforementioned Samuel, says, "Who cares about the sheriff? It's Road-Kill we need to worry about. He'll freak if he catches us knocking up his store."

"Knocking *over*, my child," Father Mike sighs, and then everyone is all of a sudden friends again.

Samuel is Samuel Clearwater, a seventeen-year-old high school senior, full-blood Ojibwe Indian, cub reporter, resort handyman, first-time offender, and, it turns out, very persuasive speaker.

Miranda is Miranda Peters, thirty-nine, a single mom with two kids, owner of a struggling resort, *another* persuasive speaker, and, I guess I should admit, my erstwhile girlfriend—"erstwhile" being the key word here.

Father Mike is simply Father Mike—an Irish priest in a small Minnesota town. His real name is Francis, but he once confided in me that neither "Father Francis" nor even the slightly more robust "Father Frank" seemed to work for the rough-and-tumble flocks of the Iron Range. What he's doing here, God only knows. No pun intended.

Me? I'm Pete Farmer, and I own the local newspaper, the Spirit Lake *Gazette*. I'd like to say that I'm here on official *Gazette* business, here to cover the breaking news (or perhaps I should say the breaking and *entering* news), but really I'm only part of this caper because Samuel and Miranda pushed me into the truck and told me I was coming. Like I said, they're both very persuasive.

We've just tumbled, like so many wet rags in a spin dryer, into the stockroom of Rand Rademacher's Coast-to-Coast hardware store. Rand is known around town as "Road-Kill" Rademacher, for reasons that will soon become apparent. His store, which we are burglar-

izing for reasons that probably *won't* become apparent (I'm not certain I understand them myself) is actually only three doors down from the offices of the *Gazette* on one side, and six doors down from the offices of the Wyatt County Sheriff's Department on the other side. It's a cozy little town we live in, Spirit Lake.

We make our way cautiously through the stockroom and into the hardware store itself. Rain beaded on the windows gives the store an underwater feel, both festive and melancholy at the same time. We huddle close, four errant fish, and strain to see if any late-night hobbyists are observing our oversized aquarium from street or sidewalk.

"Anyone with any sense is home in a nice warm bed," I say.

"I'm plenty warm right here," Miranda says. She shucks off her windbreaker and plops it onto the floor like an oversized Gore-Tex mop.

"Dry then," I sniff.

Father Mike intercedes before anything can start up between the two of us. "Let us proceed, little sheep," he says. "I do believe Ed's good brandy is finally starting to wear off."

"It *is*," Samuel says, although in reality he quaffed only a single lite beer back at his grandfather's house— hardly enough to calm the jangling nerves of a first-time petty thief.

Petty?

Certainly in the grand scheme of things, stealing a big, ugly, dead, stuffed fish must seem pretty petty. Unfortunately, Road-Kill Rademacher is not known for his belief in the grand scheme of things, and the fish in question is, technically, his.

"Why are we doing this again?" I ask, but no one answers. I'm not sure why I'm even here, although it does occur to me that I'm the only one of us with a pickup truck that actually runs.

We creep as one down the center aisle of the hardware store, sidling like crabs around a large dump bin showcasing stainless steel gardening tools and inexpensive canvas work gloves. Our quarry sits at the very front of the store—or rather hangs there, immediately above the double-wide front door and spanning a sizable section of wall from transom to ceiling.

The wall itself is a collage of odds and ends, gathered over the years by several generations of Rademachers. Some of the items are farm-oriented (a rusty plow blade, a gap-spoked wheel off some old hay buggy); others are merely weird (a moon-windowed outhouse door, a stuffed "jackelope" with perfect tiny antlers); but the vast majority are grisly tributes to what many in Spirit Lake consider Rand's only interesting personality trait.

Unlucky birds and beasts hang everywhere, frozen forever in embarrassing poses. One set of antlers racks the very Peterbilt grill that transformed deer into display. A poised-to-strike rattlesnake struggles to look formidable despite the thick Goodyear print running across its midsection. Even a beloved family setter—at least the portion of it that escaped the tines of the combine—dangles from one corner, memorialized on permanent point toward the fishing tackle in aisle twelve.

Rand has done most of the taxidermy work himself, and the results are gorier and more sordid than a professional might have achieved, but the four of us are immediately mesmerized anyway. For here, despite the macabre and sometimes cruel minutiae that surrounds it, hangs one amazing mother of a sight. Here is the fish—Old Ugly—and all any of us can do is stare with unabashed awe.

© Susanna Sharp-Schwacke, 2006

Old Ugly is a lake sturgeon. She (only the females of the species grow to such enormity) is eight feet long, two feet high at the crest of her spiny back, and in life weighed just a snail under 230 pounds. She is a monster, a nightmarish creature by anyone's standards: greenish-yellow skin, bony plates of armor covering her head and body, a tall scythe-like shark's tail, and a wide, flattened snout. On the underside of the snout is a nest of eel-like barbels from which protrudes a pinkish mouth much like the end of a vacuum cleaner hose.

"Mother of God," Father Mike says.

"My kids are never going swimming again," Miranda offers.

Each of us has seen Old Ugly by daylight, but night and the storm combine to conjure a completely new experience. Reflected rain dapples the monster's dusty hide, turning the cracking leather slick and sinewy. A flash of lightning photographs the store in brilliant blue-white, and the after-image lingers deep within the black marble eyes of the beast like some Frankenstein spark of unthinkable rebirth.

"What in the world does your grandfather want with this demon anyway?" I ask.

Samuel shines a narrow flashlight beam on a small brass plate in the corner of Old Ugly's mounting board. "Lake sturgeon (*Acipenser fulvescens*)," he reads. "Taken from Spirit Lake on August 6, 1913 by two Indian lads who trapped and drowned the beast on a sandbar."

"Doesn't name the boys, of course," says Father Mike. "Mere Indians and all."

"This fish," Samuel continues, "is the largest ever taken from Spirit Lake, and the second largest ever taken in Minnesota."

"I wonder how the poor thing ended up here," Miranda says.

Father Mike raises one bushy white eyebrow. "I believe Ed Clearwater has been wondering that himself."

Samuel blinks his flashlight off and looks at us. "How it got here is unimportant. It's ours, my grandfather wants it, and we're taking it back."

I take a deep breath and swipe one hand across my face as if to clear away any remnants of good reason. "Does this place carry ladders?" I say.

The theft itself takes only minutes. Balancing precariously on shiny aluminum step ladders, Samuel and I lower our prize to Miranda and Father Mike. Stuffed with sawdust, Old Ugly no longer weighs what she once did, but her mounting board seems inordinately heavy. It's as if the board has petrified during its time on the wall, as if the simple plank has absorbed all of the fear and sorrow of Road-Kill Rademacher's grisly hobby and transformed it into pure stone.

"Jesus!" says Father Mike. He and Miranda wobble a bit until Samuel and I are able to descend the ladders, place them back in line against the far wall, and return to help cart away our strange pirate's booty.

Outside, even the four of us together have to struggle a bit to grunt Old Ugly into the back of my pickup. I don't have a bed-liner in the truck, and the screech of the mounting board scraping across bare metal sets dogs to barking all over town.

"Nobody take off their gloves until we get back to Ed's place," Father Mike says. "And cover up the fish in case we get pulled over."

I dutifully pull a tarp over Old Ugly while Samuel tries to muscle the door of the hardware store back into place.

"We really did a number on that door," Miranda says.

Father Mike scowls momentarily at Samuel's repair work. The door looks like some mediocre boxer's front tooth, knocked askew by a poorly blocked right-hook. Father Mike signs a mysterious, vaguely Catholic gesture and sighs. "We apologize, Mr. Rademacher. May your repairs be easy and quick."

"That'll carry some weight with your review board," I say.

"Yes, well, so will stealing the damned fish."

As we drive back to Ed's house, the night begins to clear. The rain peters down into a fine drizzle and then mists out altogether An enormous full moon floats out from behind low clouds.

"*Miini-giizis,*" Samuel says. "The Blueberry Moon."

Ed sits waiting on the porch of his squat, overflowing museum of a house. He rises as I whisper the truck to a stop, and smiles broadly as, one by one, we tumble forth from the pickup like so many clowns from a tiny, bright circus car.

"Grandfather," Samuel says. "We did it."

Ed continues to stand and smile, his face etched and ravined like some sort of topographical relief map. He might be a hundred years old or a thousand, it's impossible to guess. I marvel over all of the things he must have seen in his life. I wonder how the pilfering of some ancient stuffed fish stacks up against the other amazing events he must have been witness to.

Samuel climbs into the bed of the pickup and throws back the tarp to uncover our prize. Ed whispers an ancient name, lost instantly on a breath of warm breeze, and then says, so that we all can hear, "*Miikawaadad.*"

"She's beautiful," Samuel translates.

Ed bends close to Old Ugly and whispers a string of secrets, mixing the Anishinaabemowin of his youth with English and even a word or two of delicate French he must have learned from his third wife. When he looks up again, his eyes are dark and full of mystery, but his smile shimmers with a sense of peace that cools like deep water. "*Aapji go mii gwech,*" he tells each of us in turn—thank you so very much—and his accompanying smile feels like some deeply personal, individualized gift.

This seems like a logical place to end the night's adventure, but Ed apparently has other plans. "*Zaaga'iganing,*" he says, creaking one finger toward a rutted dirt path tunneling through the trees.

"You've got to be kidding," I say. "The lake's half a mile. The truck will never make it through all that mud."

Ed's grin flashes like the iridescent sheen of a trout leaving its own universe to snatch at mayflies: the truck had never crossed his mind.

"We have to walk it," Samuel says.

"Portage the fish!" The idea fills Father Mike with inordinate glee. "There's a great sermon in there. A modern parable, I just know it."

"Yes," I say. "And you'll have plenty of time to work on it serving three-to-five for burglary down at Saint Cloud."

"An anecdote for my retirement kegger," Father Mike amends. "After the *good* Catholics have left."

"Let's do this if we're doing it," Miranda says. She is not particularly fastidious, nor even strongly inclined toward efficiency—but she does have kids to get home to, after all.

"We've come this far, we'll make it," Samuel says, and the rest of us can see—in the purposeful way he begins to wrestle the mounting board out of the pickup—the serious young brave, the *Odgidjida*, that Samuel has become over the course of the summer just past.

One by one, we join Samuel at his labor—first wrenching Old Ugly a foot at a time past the end of the pickup gate, then carefully hefting the mounting board free and up onto our shoulders. The fish—perhaps because she is no longer a prisoner of Rand's trophy wall, perhaps because she senses where destiny is leading next—seems lighter and more manageable than before. Like some strange band of nocturnal pallbearers, we carry our bizarre cargo into the forest.

We emerge from the trees twenty minutes later to find Spirit Lake glassily calm under an endless canopy of stars. Ed wades in up to his shins, shoes and all. "The water's warm," he says. He comes back and leans close to Old Ugly to translate: "*Giizhoogamin.*" We stand as if waiting for the ancient mummy to either approve or decline Ed's offer. After a moment, Samuel takes a tentative step forward and Ed nods: Old Ugly is ready.

Samuel leads the procession out into the still, dark lake. The water washes away the mud of the forest and the buzz of insect bites we hadn't even noticed until the itch disappeared. When the water is up to our waists, we gently lower the mounting board and let it float. The board bobs languidly for a moment and then catches an invisible current. It swirls lazily through unseen eddies and along some secret channel toward the center of the lake.

"*Booch igo ingoding giga-nagishkodaadimin,*" Ed calls from shore. He smiles as we all gather around him. "I told her we would meet again sometime."

"Not soon," Samuel says. "Let it be a long time yet."

Miini-giizis drops below the treeline on the far horizon, and the sky turns first pink and then salmon and then blossoms into a magnificent dawn. With the sunrise comes a brisk, insistent wind—a hint of autumn goosing the dog days of summer out of their languor. On a morning so clear, the view across Spirit Lake seems endless, yet there is no sign of Old Ugly.

"She must have sunk," I say.

Ed looks at me and smiles.

We return to Ed's place for breakfast, giddy from too much adventure and too little sleep. Ed brings out fresh blueberries and maple cornbread, brews strong chicory coffee, offers up strips of salty smoked whitefish that taste somehow of autumn and childhood and Christmas and April all at once. Ed builds a small bonfire, and we eat and laugh and watch spirits gambol in the smoke of the burning wood.

On my way home, I drive past one of the many small public boat landings that dot the shores of Spirit Lake. I see something out of the corner of my eye that makes me slam both feet down onto the brake pedal without even thinking. Luckily no one is behind me. I pull a messy U-turn and bump down into the access area.

There's Old Ugly's mounting board, big as life, bobbing upside-down a few feet out from shore. The sheriff or the game warden could be by at any minute. Or some fisherman, loading in his boat for a day on the lake. Even Rand Rademacher himself—he probably passes by this very spot on his way to work every morning.

I get out of the truck and wade into the water. Maybe I can push Old Ugly under and weigh her down with something. Or maybe I can push her over into the reeds and cattails, hide her until I can bring Samuel back to help move her somewhere more permanent. I reach for the board, and realize that it hasn't been floating up-side-down at all. The brass plate in the corner of the wood glints in the morning sun. The rest of the board is empty save for a monstrous dark outline in the center of the faded wood.

I think about this for a moment. A few yards out from where I stand, something big and dark rolls the surface of the water, but it's gone before I really even see it. Huge concentric circles roll outward from the spot, but soon even they are just a memory.

I finally look down and discover that the mounting board has once again taken off on its own unknowable current. It's too far out for me to reach without

swimming, and I wouldn't know what to do with it once I'd captured it anyway.

I get back in my truck and drive into town. I stop at Tiny's Diner, where people are already buzzing about last night's break-in at the Coast-to-Coast. Rand, from all accounts, is livid—and understandably so. The sheriff is apparently less concerned—he's sitting at the counter, quietly eating an omelet.

Someone hollers over that they expect a big write-up in next week's *Gazette*. I smile and wave, then wonder how in the world I'm ever going to write this one. I can write about the break-in, of course, that's no problem. But the real story?

A priest, an Indian, a reporter, and a single mom walk into a hardware store—it sounds like the beginning of some silly bar joke. Even if I wrote it, who could ever take it seriously?

Besides, everyone around these parts has heard this chestnut a million times before. It's really just a fish story, isn't it? Another whopper about the big one that got away. ◆▪◆

© Mildred Figueroa, 2006

GRAIN ELEVATORS
SILK SCREENS & PHOTOGRAPHS
BECKY DICKERSON

Grand Rapids Elevator

Haskins Elevator

Sugar Ridge Elevator

Elevator

© Becky Dickerson, 2006

© Becky Dickerson, 2006

© Becky Dickerson, 2006

MY MILITARY-INDUSTRIAL COMPLEX

GARY BUSLIK

The check-in line at José Marti International was for tourists what every other line in Cuba was for Cubans: long and languid and as listless as a python after eating an agouti on a sweltering afternoon. We had sclerosed for almost two hours—sitting on our suitcases, reading, playing blackjack, muttering obscenities, occasionally standing to regain circulation and nudge our bags with our feet, playing Name That Tune on zippers and Hang the Butcher, with the Butcher sporting a beard, smoking a cigar, and wearing guerilla fatigues from the 1950s. But, like the Dow Industrial Average, in all that time we had gotten absolutely nowhere. One crummy check-in agent for a couple of hundred sunburned, bunion-throbbing, pissed-off Yanquis. Eventually the python began to bulge here and there and then break apart like on that New Hampshire Revolutionary flag, "Live Free or Die."

When I couldn't stand it anymore, I moseyed outside and found a kid—Raphael, nine years old—selling stale coconut fragments and gave him ten dollars to come inside and stand in line for me.

Let me explain something. In Cuba you can bribe anyone to do anything for a U.S. dollar. One night we went to the Museum of the Revolution, only to find it closed for "remodeling"—a term that is to Cuban economic reality what "international" is to Cuban airport. Well, fine. One dollar, and the security guard not only let us in and turned on the lights, he invited us to help ourselves to whatever mementos we might like, such as *Granma*, the boat on which Castro and a hundred of his men sailed from Mexico to launch their revolution. "Go on," he said, waving, "just take it."

If you got sick on hotel food and—the Cuban doctors being among the world's best—they diagnosed you with needing an entire upper-body transplant, and there were three thousand desperately ill Cubans on the upper-body waiting list, a buck would do the trick, and you'd be flying home with a spanking new thorax.

So in offering Raphael a sawbuck, I was not only giving him at least a thousand times more than necessary, I was also single-handedly reviving the Cuban gross domestic product. Unfortunately my wife didn't see it that way.

"What's the matter with you?" she hissed.

I explained about the Cuban economy.

"He's not standing in line for you. It's demeaning."

"Not as demeaning as constantly losing at Hang the Butcher. What the hell kind of a word is *sphygmomanometer*? You made that up."

"Not you. Demeaning for *him*, you twit."

"Now there's a word I can wrap my brain around."

"Send him back out there."

"He's selling chunks of old coconuts for a nickel. He'll be dead before he makes ten bucks."

"Then let him keep the ten dollars."

"It's not slavery. He wants to work for it. Look," I said, "if you send him away, he'll think it's his fault. Anyhow, what's so demeaning about standing in line?" I glanced around at our fellow travelers. "I'll bet they wish they'd thought of it first." She magnetized my molecules with her MRI glare—usually reserved for when George Bush says something idiotic, as if I, personally, had been responsible for the low oxygen level in his incubator. "Hey, we all work for someone."

"Not standing in line for spoiled Americans," she said.

A fat Canadian with a ponytail in front of us shook his head—in disgust, if I wasn't mistaken. "Right on, sister," he muttered. Instead of a respectable, bourgeois suitcase with gimpy wheels, he nudged a backpack across the floor, the kind usually seen on the bony shoulders of pimply college undergraduates, not middle-aged men shaped like Shamu the whale. I knew he was an escapee from the Great White North because his passport was tucked into a strap on his backpack, as if he wanted to make damn well sure everyone knew he wasn't an American. You can pick out a Canadian passport from across a room, because it is gray, like their country, and its cover features a gold-embossed portrait of Queen Elizabeth eating a bacon sandwich. You can tell it's bacon by the curlicue tail sticking out of the bread.

I happen to like Canadians. Many years ago, my best friend, Steve, and I spent a week at a fly-in fishing camp in southern Ontario, on a system of lakes that, had Livingston been fishing there, Stanley would not have found him in a bazillion years. The landscape was so unremittingly wet and featureless and bland, even Canadians considered it boring. It was like a Hamm's Beer bar sign had fallen off the wall into the sink, and the bartender accidentally left the cold faucet running overnight, and a storm came and blew the roof off the bar, and the bartender, who had fallen asleep drunk in the storeroom, drowned.

The lakes were so easy to get lost on that we were supposed to wear bright orange ponchos so the seaplane that had dropped us off would be able to find us in a week, and if we heard the plane but didn't see it, we were supposed to make a fire and, if necessary, burn all our clothing to attract attention. The problem being that we and all of our belongings were so thoroughly soaked to the bone—if our belongings had had bones—that we could have doused ourselves with kerosene from our sleeping-bag warmers—had we not run out of kerosene four days earlier, and had our sleeping bags not fallen out of our capsized canoe, along with our food, tent, clothes, and ourselves—and they still would not have caught fire.

So we wound up fishing naked, which we found liberating and glorious and spiritual, until my accident with the lure. Then we had to call for an air ambulance, which cost three thousand dollars Canadian—sixty-five dollars U.S.—but which at least supplied us with dry hospital gowns. They flew us to Winnipeg, where they surgically removed the lure and related minnow, and, after a massive dose of antibiotics, we saw an American movie with Canadian subtitles and went to a "massage" parlor where we could be with actual women, as opposed to walleye pikes dressed up like women. My "massage therapist" was a nifty brunette named Margo, who at the time reminded me of Jill St. John, but in retrospect more resembled Herbert Hoover. In any event, there I was lying on my back, "massage" towel draped over groin, and Margo dribbling warm "massage" oil into my navel while we engaged in preparatory idle chitchat. Then she asked me if I would like her to remove the towel, and I said sure, and when she saw what was underneath she screamed and asked what the hell was that. I told her it was a fish-hook accident, but I don't think she believed me because she blew a whistle, and in ran a seven-foot-tall Canadian with a hockey stick who threatened to slap-shot me stupid if I did not scram and take my weird-looking groin and my friend Steve with me. Or it may have been the other way around.

So you might wonder why I like Canadians, and I will tell you. A couple of years later the Blackhawks made it to the Stanley Cup playoffs versus the Maple Leafs, and who should turn out to be Toronto's star defenseman but Matt Powell, Margo's seven-foot bouncer. I had just met Janice, and I wanted to impress her on our first date, so I asked her if she wanted to go to a playoff game, only to find out that tickets were pretty much impossible to get. So in desperation I found out what bar the players hung out at, and I took a chance and cornered Powell, and after very little prodding he remembered that I was the fish-hook guy whose arm he had threatened to tear off and beat me with, and I bought him a Labatt beer, and we became new best friends. He got me two front-row seats, and Janice thought I was some kind of CEO or something, and I asked Powell not to mention the Margo/lure incident in front of her, and he never did. So we fell in love—me and Janice, not me and the defenseman—and I thought she was a Republican, so I married her.

And she was a Republican, too, until George W. Bush got elected, at which time she became a communist, and now she blames me personally for everything that comes out of his mouth, including the hay.

Somehow or other it was *my* fault that we didn't find weapons of mass destruction in Iraq, that the levees failed in New Orleans, that there was a volcanic eruption on Montserrat, and that Karl Rove is the moral equivalent of smog. I am not allowed to watch Fox News while she is in the room or turn off any TV while set to that station, in case she should be the first to turn it on again. She is suddenly gung-ho for Hugo Chavez, reparations for blacks, and changing Chief Illiniwek's name to Chief Rotten Imperialist Pig. She now believes that *The Wall Street Journal* is an example of ideological state apparatus; that maybe Thomas Jefferson wasn't such a great guy after all, considering he liked brown booty; that Fidel Castro is the second coming—assuming there had been a first, which she doubts—and if George Bush had his way, Havana would be a Wal-Mart and the rest of Cuba a parking lot, as though the previous fifty years have been a figment of the earth's imagination. She tosses the word *hegemony* around like beer cans at a picnic trash container—usually missing.

Reminding her that she had married me under possibly false pretenses fell on "audibly disadvantaged" ears, and she replied that if I wanted a divorce, fine and dandy, and if Bushy nominated one more evangelical Christian lunkhead to the Supreme Court, she had her divorce lawyer, Adolph Hitler Mendelbaum, ready to file, so I'd better pray for the justices' good health.

So, yes, I did like Canadians, but the muttering former hippie in front of us at José Marti "International" was a tad suspicious-seeming. For one thing, I had seldom seen a fat Canadian—they worked off their bacon by cleaning fish, I guess—and, for another thing, all the hippies I had ever known pretty much grew out of it in their twenties, when they traded in their roach clips for Audis and condos. The last time I had seen a ponytail on a man the age of this so-called Canadian was when they found that Green Beret alive in the Cambodian jungle, having survived there for thirty years and never knowing the war was over or that Nixon had resigned and that America had matured to the point where we would teach creationism again in our public schools, and all he could eat was capybara poop until long and intense psychotherapy, during which he was gradually introduced to current movie prices and "The O'Reilly Factor."

So right off the bat I didn't like this corpulent, time-warped freakazoid, although based on what you already know about my wife, you probably thought she would have answered his clearly provocative, anti-American crack, "Right on, sister," with a raised-fist, black-power salute, like those putzes in the 1968 summer Olympics whose names no one even remembers, and that she would have given him a hippie handshake and trucked-on-down with him to the airport lounge, where they would have shared carrot juice and a toke, and they would have exchanged notes on how to blow up oil tankers.

You would think so, but you would be as wrong as a naked fisherman trying desperately to reel in a twelve-hook, Godzilla-brand lure that happened to be snagged on a sunken Canadian log. You cannot get more wrong.

Because here is an interesting thing about Janice. On the one hand, she will make a mad dash to Michael Moore's latest movie with the enthusiasm of one dog's nose up another dog's poo-poo, and she will return home spewing all manner of liberal claptrap to her emotionally needy, Bush-voting husband who desperately wants a bit of nooky before bedtime. On the other hand, you can't make a sow's ear out of a silk purse, and I knew, just *knew*, that when it came down to it, if some foreign, Jefferson Airplane-loving weed-sucker dared to say peep against her country, she would de-spleen him with the efficiency of mongoose on snake.

And sure enough, recognizing that murderous, patriotic gleam in her eye, I both feared for the unsuspecting, pony-tailed lard bucket and, at the same time, braced myself for some yuks.

But, oddly, she pinged him with only a grazing look and said nothing. Instead, she turned to Raphael, folded his hand around my ten dollars, so he knew he could keep it, then pointed to the door and smiled maternally. "It's yours, honey. Go."

The kid looked at me, confused. "No change," he stuttered—probably a phrase he had learned phonetically.

Janice shook her head. *It's okay, keep it.*

Again, Raphael, frowning, glanced at me.

"No problemo," I said, loud and slow and showing my palms. "Keepo itto."

The Canadian clacked his tongue, flicked his ponytail, and rolled his pork-loving eyeballs.

Okey-dokey. Now he was really in for it. True, Janice had been perfectly willing to deal him a beginner's good hand. It had been his lucky day. He had pulled a pair of tens. But with that clacking he had pressed that luck, split his pair, and was about to get his head handed to him. He was about to be blonded.

I held my breath. This was it. Cobra, prepare to die.

She turned to me. "Fork over a twenty."

"Twenty what?"

Her eyes bulged. I whipped out my wallet and found a double sawbuck. She snapped it nice and loud—to irritate our Canadian enemy, I assumed. She handed the money to Raphael. "For you," she said. "You don't have to do anything. We have lots."

"We do?" I whispered, making a sound like a sneezing hamster.

She motioned for my wallet again.

"Um, don't you think this is the kind of thing we should discuss as a couple?"

She thrust out her palm and wriggled her fingers malevolently—again, undoubtedly for the benefit of our northern friend.

I handed her my wallet. She went right for the hidden pocket, where I kept my bail money. She handed Raphael two crisp hundreds. "For you to do whatever you want, sweet boy. Don't forget the rest of your family."

The Canadian said nothing. Evidently humiliated, demoralized, and defeated, he had returned to his crossword puzzle.

Janice took out two more hundreds from their leather lair, creased them lengthwise, and tucked them into the lad's pocket. "We're rich," she told him. "Wealthy Americans. Very spoiled." She turned to me. "Aren't we, dear?"

I cleared my throat. She handed me back my wallet with three dollars in it.

Did we show that Canadian, or what?! *These colors don't run!*

She patted Raphael's head. "Have a nice day."

The boy turned to me. I could see what was left of his lunch on his back teeth. Coconut.

"Yeah, have a nice day," I said. "Try real hard."

Janice tilted her head at me. I held up my hand. "Okay, I'm not saying another word."

"And you're going to keep me company in line and not get any more bright ideas?"

"You bet, and no way."

"Deal the cards, bright boy."

I did, and she drew twenty-one, and I busted. We sat on two suitcases and used the third as a table, and every now and then we'd inch along and continue playing, and after about an hour I dealt her a ten and a six and was waiting for her to indicate stay or hit, and when she didn't I glanced up and saw her looking around the hall, her mouth twisted weirdly, her eyebrows gnarled, and I followed her gaze and saw it too. I was the last one to see it, but that's the story of my life.

Raphael had put out the word, had rounded up a horde of his young *compañeros*, or whatever they're called, who were stampeding the waiting line with offers to stand in for passengers at a U.S. dollar each. In a few minutes Janice and I were pretty much the only non-Cubans still in line—the Canadian having been one of the first to fork over his buck—no doubt so he could rout up a pork sandwich.

It all worked out, though. I taught the urchins how to play blackjack, and when they lost their money, I explained about what we call in English the "learning curve" and made them repeat the phrase several times until you could hardly detect an accent, and after I won back my bail money, I let them play on credit, and when they continued to lose I was willing to let them work off their debt by walking on Janice's and my backs, which were killing us from having waited so long in line. At first she didn't like the idea, but when I pointed out that I was teaching them the evils of gambling, ancillary to the evils of capitalism, she, too, saw it as a life-lesson master stroke and flipped over on her tummy. ◆▪◆

MIDWEST LIFE
IN THE CITY
AS OBSERVED BY
LORAIN COUNTY
COMMUNITY COLLEGE
PHOTOGRAPHY STUDENTS

© Brittany Parfitt, 2006

© Brittany Parfitt, 2006

© Brittany Parfitt, 2006

© Danielle Grodek, 2006

© Danielle Grodek, 2006

© Mark Chambers, 2006

IKEA AND ME
(A MIDWESTERN WRITER'S SEARCH FOR THE SCANDINAVIAN MUSE)
SARA JANE RATTAN

Finally, I am at my desk. A desk that I fought to build. Not like my grandfather might have built a thing, carefully choosing the best tool to plane a surface or to miter a corner. Nor even like my father, who once or twice improvised a small piece to please my mother, a side table or a shelf, something with unusual dimensions not easily found in our town's department store or the Penney's catalog. Unlike my father and my grandfather before him, I did not work with raw lumber or without plans. I fought and clawed and struggled with a kit.

Buoyed by the optimism and confidence that so often attach at a venture's outset, I hauled what appeared to be a corrugated coffin into the house and up the steps to a corner of our bedroom that I regard as "my study." I opened one end of the box, only to find that I could not see the pieces of my desk. They were hidden from sight, firmly ensconced in deftly packed Styrofoam casings whose extraction from the box flew in the face of all accepted principles of physics and gravity. It took several non-surgical strikes with a pair of box cutters to free the casings, and I carefully laid out each of the numbered pieces of pressed wood, covered with cherry veneer, that would somehow coalesce into the simple writing table pictured on the box. There were sixty-three. It seemed a large number for a table with four legs and two shallow drawers.

Where to begin? I shook a batch of nuts and bolts free from their plastic wrappings. They came to rest and lay immobile on the bubble wrap, not unlike the odd assortment of insects that used to collect on the Shell No-Pest Strips nailed to the wall in the service station near my grandfather's house.

The bolts were squat, ugly twisted things, as repulsive as water bugs, not the pale inelegant creatures that skitter across the surface of sun warmed ponds, but the shiny, bulging black beetle-like crawlies that emerge from the underbellies of paint-flecked radiators and leaky sinks. Inert, the bolts did not trigger the same horror as their insect kin, but they sat–all the same–leering at me, next to pressed wood pieces #23 and #24, the two mitered boards that would form one of the corners of my desk.

The corner's assembly clearly required a second person, a husband, preferably of the handy, treehouse building, "can do," "no problem, I can fix that" variety. However, I would have to content myself with the *other* type: the computer-bound, happy to make waffles, endlessly patient with small boys but lacking *all* of the aforementioned qualities and "make no apologies for it" variety. A lawyer.

My enthusiasm was waning. Rapidly.

I had started out believing that the desk's assembly would require only a short time, one hour or perhaps two, and that I would have as many chapters in hand by the end of the day–written out in long-hand, arm moving smoothly–no, effortlessly–across the desk's shining cherry veneer surface. The desk would by my muse, a wellspring of inspiration. But clearly, as the scattered sheets of instructions and unfixed bolts reminded me, the desk's assembly would not be brief or uncomplicated.

In the days that followed, the temperature climbed and I avoided the jumble of unconnected wooden boards and metal crosspieces with the same determination that I avoid untangling snarled hair on a small child or a kinked chain in the corner of a jewelry box. Such tangles can be avoided until the hair requires smoothing or the necklace must be worn. When, I wondered, would I need to write?

My husband was in no hurry to climb the stairs and contemplate the jumbo over-sized wooden puzzle that lay neglected on the floor of our bedroom. This was the Midwest, did he need to remind me? Where spring passes in a heartbeat and where steamy summer mornings are just a memory by the time the yard has been mowed a half dozen times and the hollyhocks have gone to seed. At day's end, the front porch was my husband's destination. And, without too much encouragement, I joined him. Upstairs, pressed wood pieces #23 and #24 continued to lie fallow in a field of short shag carpet.

At night, we picked our way among the pieces, wending our way to bed like children on worm-puddled sidewalks. Incipient poems raged in my head. Unreleased, I was convinced, only for want of a simple writing table. Occasionally, I reflected (with no small degree of discomfort) on Annie Dillard's words: "How we spend our days is, of course, how we spend our lives." Judged in those terms, the currency of my writing days was beginning to dwindle.

The days grew longer. The sun lingered overhead after dinner and the boys played outside while we rinsed the dishes. Later, we listened to them shouting to one another, their voices ringed with the sound of summer elation, the elation of children running in the dark, among shapes that loom deliciously large in the street lamp's shadows. Whole mornings were spent on bikes, escorting them to story hours and Little League practice, stopping at the green grocer to pick out bundles of basil and shiny peppers the color of stop-and-go lights. Not a bad way to spend a string of hot summer days. Perhaps,

I reflected from my seat on the porch, they might have a currency of their own–even in Annie Dillard's eyes.

Still, the cherry veneer beckoned.

Three Saturdays had come and gone, and I began to worry that pressed wood pieces #23 and #24 would soon find their way to a game of stickball or to the map room of our sons' backyard fort if we did not bolt them into their proper place.

So I rose early one Saturday and prepared a fine breakfast. Upon finishing his eggs and toast, my husband capitulated. "Okay, let's go take a look at the desk." We climbed the stairs. I was pleased and impressed by the determination in my own step. I could feel the beginning of the song in my head, the song calling out the poems and stories that had scattered like children at the kicking of the can. But our good intentions would come to naught: these were no ordinary bolts, my bulging black crawlies. *These* bolts required a vise grip.

We had owned a vise grip at one time or another, of that I was sure. But there was no sign of it in our small toolbox. I could call "ollie ollie oxen free" all that I wanted, but I stood alone: no vise grip or poems in sight. Our tool box had long been emptied of almost all things useful by our fort-building, kick-the-can playing, "a vise grip looks just like a laser gun, doesn't it?" offspring.

"I'll go to the hardware store."

"I'll be on the porch."

On the way out, I stubbed my toe on some yet to be identified cross piece. Drat Annie Dillard, anyway!

We somehow managed to assemble the desk by week's end. But the poems did not answer the muse's call. I polished the cherry veneer. It looked inviting, but the invitation went unanswered. Only unclaimed laundry and three stray socks chanced the desk's pristine surface. Their claim proved tenacious. New piles of laundry appeared as quickly as I cleared away their predecessors; like an invasive, non-native species, a wild growth of tangled underwear and swim trunks quickly choked the yet to be explored cherry plains that lay beneath. If this were a clearing at Tinker's Creek, Dillard's neighbors might well have recommended the unthinkable: a controlled burn.

Inside, this was impracticable.

Vigilance was the only weapon left me in my crusade.

I uprooted shorts and stray socks as quickly as they cropped up, encouraging the boys to shed whatever they were wearing *before* plunging into the sprinkler or the mud puddle at the back of our garage.

Miraculously, I began to pull ahead.

A more seasoned writer would have known to plant a cover crop, to lay out a journal or a second draft. But, heady with my own success, I began to use the surface–one of the few clear horizontal surfaces in the house–to sort through receipts and tax returns, a project of much longer standing than the laundry.

Now, it is October. All the receipts are filed and our boys spend the evenings inside. During the day, they are safely tucked in school. I can sit undisturbed and listen to the sounds of autumn's first chill breezes and to the flocks of restless songbirds, swooping the skies outside my window. The vise grip is safely nestled in the tool box. I will be sure to kiss my husband tonight. But now, I sit, pen poised above a table top clear of tax returns and unmatched socks. I don't wait for the muse. I just begin. It's time to lay down a cover crop, to till the fields. And just as I knew she would, the muse follows, calling out to me as I revel in the cleared acres of cherry veneer that stretch out all around me: "Mommm… what's for dinner?" ❖❖❖

© Susanna Sharp-Schwacke, 2006

TATTOO
MARK PUTZI

```
On                                                    the
   back of                                        your lucky
      left shoulder                           where you see
         only in reflection,                 my needle exposes
            an intoxicated man's      2   maculate square inches
               (A pictograph—      The      fulcrum between
                  colossal good    and      evil, not truth
                  but luck!)        in       haphazard
               calligraphy.      After   all does not
                  a lucky        man      create
                     his         own      truth?
                                 And
                                 do
            you smile or cry when
               for $15 and    30    minutes we
               collaborate:    I   who stoically
               transcribe, and    you who provide
            exquisite canvas?      Your black diamond
            eyes shine as they      sample flash from
            the display case       and you smile like
            a Sufi.  "Oh,             what have you
         done?" Nothing            more than employ
         your servant                 to express
            desire                       and
            illustrate                innocence.
```

JUNGLE BOOK
MICHAEL WALDECKI

The fluorescent pale moon
floating in the summer night's sky
over south Amherst
beneath the scattered hemlocks
piecemeal along the vertical ridges
of the calm flow
of the Vermilion River.

You now recall them
the craggy splotch
poised over the still unpopulated
Firelands where I found
an American grave marker.
I keep the information from everyone,
even Jack, the historian on the
First American Revolution.
Jack consoled me with the news
the remains were now properly buried.
Things like that are odd, you see.
For forty years I drank at the pebble pool.
I didn't want to concern anyone.

As inconspicuous as the death of a sparrow—
as many times I've died, how many times was it so?
I often have hoped for an easy and peaceful death.
I believe I've traveled and died far too long.

The worm that eats this nation is called
mammon, the name of its nation is
abomination.
No wonder Vietnam was called
the Green Machine…
God help those who died bravely for lies.

LAST WORD
SAMMY GREENSPAN

When in doubt, have the pie
first.

In lieu of another cup of coffee
or that tumbler of gin, walk by the lake,
preferably with large dogs.

Run an extra mile if it helps quiet your mind.
Scrub grout or the kitchen floor. Whatever derails
the freight train of ruminating despair,
throw the switch.

By first light, let the earth cradle you
like a mother, dew-damp grass and clotted soil
between your toes. Lie down where the sky
fills your eyes. Let solitude open
the space for love.

Trust the kindness of gravity. What comes down
will bounce up again, if at times crookedly. Altitude
is relative. It's all spinning through space, after all.
No wonder we get dizzy.

Between real tears
and a good belly laugh, choose laughter,
but love the real, all its faces.

Keep the knives stowed out of sight
and the guns in somebody else's house.

Know by heart
the way to the quiet clearing in the woods
and a friend's phone number.

Feel the heartbeat of the planet
pulse up through your soles. Love
the real.

A POEM FOR LIZ
MARCE WOOD

My friend Liz is born of the sun and the lake
She's an artist,
she comes from a long line of fisher people.
She has the sparkle of the lake inside her
in a way I have never seen in anyone else,
It pours out of her

Her hair is the color of energy
it is made of Sunlight
a gift of her great great grandmother,
who is the lake

Liz knows all the birds
Mighty heron, mallard duck, sweet chick chickadee

She knows all the trees,
handsome white pine, sacred cedar, spruce
and humble balsam

The aurora borealis, can you believe it?
she knows each magnificent ribbon by name!

Liz has night time dreams full of owl,
and wolf howl,
black bear lumberings,
and craggly trees,
and massive rock walls

But the fish people are her best friends.
She says
"I know their sparkle language, they sing me songs of time
they are so clever, they just make up the words as they go along!
Did you know that? They're my closest relatives"

Liz laughs with a belly full of joy,
skinny cousin to Buddha.
She is wickedly funny because wise ones often are.

MORE
JANE K. KRETSCHMANN

To start the flow of poetry I move.
Walking my dog works—the steady pace
of six feet on asphalt, concrete, grass,
the rhythm of heel and toe, go and come,
churns the cream of my thoughts
into words I mouth:
>*My husband laments*
>*that since I've taken up writing*
>*poetry*
>*I ask the strangest questions*
>>Moving around
the house, putting away laundry,
I taste tidbits of lines,
>*and smile for no reason*
licking them like mixing spoons.
>He cannot imagine
>*that the sheer joy*
>*of writing a poem*
>*is like having your breast*
>*touched—*
Filling a notebook
I go from room to room
>*that moment when everything*
>*is possible,*
>*when you know*
>*you will live forever*
or stand, like Thomas Wolfe
at his refrigerator, hungry.

BECAUSE A FAMOUS POET TOLD ME NOT TO
EMILY BOBO

I like to write poems
with vehicles in them.
"I'm from New York."
Expecting this to be reason
enough and proof that she
knew what she was doing.
"A car's a car." Reason
enough and proof that she's
never rode a 300-horse
Dodge Windsor Golden Lion
through a Kansas grassland
littered with red and white-
topped silos; never learned
to curry rust off
a dappled gray Saab or
prod a spunky palomino
Beetle on to the next
watering hole with a
rubber band in a hailstorm;
never distinguished the feel
of leather reigns from steel
steering wheel; never
connected the foot pedal
to the spur, or the bit
to the carburetor.

JAMES WRIGHT'S LIFELINE AND BIBLIOGRAPHY
LARRY SMITH

[Originally prepared by Larry Smith for "James Wright's Ohio" video docu-drama 1988; supplemented by biographical detail from *A Wild Perfection: The Selected Letters of James Wright*, eds. Anne Wright & Saundra Rose Maley. The photos are courtesy of Liberty Kovacs and Annie Wright.]

"I was born in Ohio/ I still dream of home."

James Arlington Wright began life as one of the working poor along the beautiful and industrial Ohio River Valley. Wright struggled with his intense and ambivalent feelings for family and place most of his life. His intellectual brilliance (said to have a photographic mind) and search for larger meaning compounded that struggle. He also endured mental disorders…obsessive compulsive, manic-depressive, alcoholism…which he may have inherited from his mother Jessie. These struggles were kept secret by his circle of friends until his death. And yet his poems reveal such beautiful and tender statements of strength and survival…*This Branch Will Not Break.* His teaching was another way of 'giving back' to the world he left. His later travels with Annie to Europe bore echoes of his Ohio homeland. While facts alone cannot tell a whole story, they can reveal a path. Reading his poems, the letters now, and a biographical sketch begins to tell a larger story of his life and work.

1920's

Wright family is working-class with mother's family from West Virginia hills.

"My family was a bunch of singing drunks and good carpenters."

Father, Dudley, is a die-cutter at Hazel-Atlas Glass in Wheeling, WV. Mother, Jessie (Lyons) Wright, works at White Swan Laundry in Wheeling. Both had to quit school to earn income for their families.

1927- Dec. 13, James is born, the second of three sons: Ted, James, and Jack. Older adopted sister is Marge. Family is living in Aetnaville, south end of Martins Ferry, Ohio.

Grandmother, Elizabeth Lyons, is a comfort to James who praises her for her "anarchic humor" and loving spirit.

Ted, James & Marge on front porch in Martins Ferry, 1928.

AREA INDUSTRIES: Laughlin Steel Wheeling-Pitt Steel, La Belle Lumber, Hanna Mines, Belmont Brewery, Blaw-Knox.

POEMS TREATING THIS ERA: "Youth," "My Grandmother's Ghost, "A Centenary Ode…" and prose, "Childhood Sketch" and "The Infidel" in *Collected Prose.*

1930's

The Great Depressioin. The Wright family moves about often in the rich ethnic mix of neighborhoods in Martins Ferry.

James' youthful activities: walking in nature, swimming in the Ohio River (witnesses drowning of a young friend caught in a 'suck hole.') Figure of John Shunk emerges, diver for lost bodies in the river; joins Boy Scouts—Flying Eagles of Troop 62.

1936- Great Ohio River Flood, WPA swimming pool is dug in Martins Ferry city park by Wright relatives.

1938- James begins to write poems, influence by James Whitcomb Riley and Lord Byron.

POEMS TREATING THIS ERA: "Stages of a Journey Westward," Old Bud," "Willy Lyons," "Arts Poetica," "The Ice House," "Sumac in Ohio," "An Offering to Mr. Bluehart," "A Note Left in Jimmy Leonard's Shack," "Twilights," "The Flying Eagles of Troop 62," "On a Phrase from Southern Ohio," "Ohio Patoral," "Beautiful Ohio," "A Flower Passage," "Many of Our Waters."

1940's

James attends Shreve High School in Martins Ferry—active in track, Hi-Y, National Honor Society, International Club, *Ferrian* Yearbook staff.

1942- James misses a year of school due to "nervous breakdown" and tensions at home with mother. Grandmother Elizabeth Lyons dies.

1943- James meets Liberty Kardules in English class, girl from Greek "Bottoms" area.

TEACHERS: Helen McNeely Sheriff (Latin) and Elizabeth Willerton Esterly (English) who become influence and encourage his talents with language.

1946- Graduates from Shreve High School and enlists

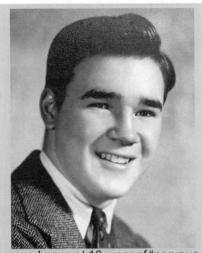
James at 16, year of "nervous breakdown, " misses school year.

James in Military occupation forces in Japan following bombing, 1946.

in the U.S. Army, trains in engineering school at Fort Lewis, Washington; serves 18 months in occupational forces in Japan; falls in love with girl in Japan, is discharged in 1947.

1948- Returns home where his family has moved to a small farm in Warnock, OH, near Martins Ferry. Enrolls in Kenyon College under G.I. Bill, studies English with John Crowe Ransom, Charles Coffin, Philip Timberlake; befriends fellow students, Roberty Mezey, E.L. Doctorow, Gene Pugatch, Roger Hecht. While at Kenyon does country & western radio show "The Great Speckled Bird." He tries working at Hazel-Atlas Glass one summer, alongside of father, but quits after one week to paint highway bridges in Ohio.

POEMS TREATING THIS ERA: "Miners," "Autumn Begins in Martins Ferry," "In Response to a Rumor…" "What Are You Going to Do," "In Memory of Charles Coffin"

1950's

1950- Friendship with Liberty (Libby) turns to romance; they become engaged in 1951.

1952- Writes for Kenyon's *HIKA* literary magazine and wins school's Robert Frost Poetry Prize, graduates magna cum laude in January with thesis on Thomas Hardy; February he and Liberty marry in Greek Orthodox Church in Martins Ferry. That summer they move to Philadelphia where Liberty works as nurse and James works on the railroad. In August he receives Fulbright Fellowship to study German literature at University of Vienna in

James and Liberty wedding celebration at her parents' home in Martins Ferry.

Austria, where he discovers the poetry of George Trakl and Theodore Storm.

1953- Son Franz is born in Vienna; they return home by way of Germany and London, then spend the summer with family in Ohio.

1954- James studies at the University of Washington in Seattle with Theodore Roethke and Stanley Kunitz; fellow student friends are Carolyn Kizer, Richard Hugo, David Waggoner.

1957- Receives M.A. degree and begins Ph.D. in English literature; he wins a series of poetry prizes including the Yale Younger Poets Award for first book *The Green Wall* (Yale Univ. Press.) Wright is influenced by Thomas Hardy and Robert Frost; he explains that title is to suggest the walls of the Ohio Valley he had to climb out of. He is denied a teaching position at Univ. of Washington, and so begins teaching at Univ. of Minnesota (1957-1964) and later at Macalister College in St. Paul, MN. Corresponding with James Dickey, Robert Bly, and Donald Hall, among others.

Liberty and James in Vienna, she is pregnant with Franz. 1953.

James holding Franz at Mt. Si, Washington, 1954.

1958- Son Marshall is born in MN. Period of personal and marital turbulence, heavy drinking, trial separation. Liberty and James are both receiving psychiatric treatment. Liberty attends classes at Univ. of Minnesota; James is depressed and obsessive-compulsive over his being in Minnesota..

James befriends Robert and Carol Bly and spends time at their Odin House in Madison, MN. James begins to work with Bly and John Knoepfle on translations of German and South American poets.

1959- Receives Ph.D. from Univ. of Washington for study "The Comic Imagination of the Young Dickens"; does public readings of his work. Works on translations

James, Minneapolis, 1958.

Robert Bly, James Wright, and Louis Simpson at Bly's farm in Madison, MN.

James and Annie (Runk) Wright, Chicago 1967.

of Spanish and Latin American poets. Publishes *Saint Judas* (Wesleyan Univ. Press).
POEMS TREATING THIS ERA: "A Minnesota Poem," "Bay a Lake in Minnesota," "Lying in a Hammock at William Duffy's Farm in Pine Island, Minnesota," "Milkweed," "A Blessing." "To an Evening Star in Central Minnesota," "To a Girl Heavy with Child"

1960's

1960- Twenty Poems of Georg Trakl (Sixties Press) translated with Robert Bly. Teaches summer courses at Moorhead State, outside Fargo, North Dakota.
1962- James is godfather to Mary Bly; spends time relaxing and writing at Bly farm. Liberty graduates from Univ. of Minnesota with a degree in nursing (later earns Ph.D. in family counseling). Divorce from Liberty; she takes sons to live in San Francisco. James retracts book "Amenities of Stone" from Wesleyan Press.
1963- The Branch Will Not Break (Wesleyan, revision of "Amenities of Stone"); *Twenty Poems of Cesar Vallejo* (Sixties Press) translated with Bly and Knoepfle.

Denied tenure of University of Minnesota, he begins teaching at Macalester College in Saint Paul.
1964- Riders of a White Horse by Theodore Storm, translated by James Wright.
1965- Guggenheim Award, visits Elizabeth Willerton in California; spends several months living with parents near Martins Ferry

James teaching at Hunter College, NYC 1968.

James on horse David at Bly farm, photo by Carol Bly.

1966- Begins teaching at Hunter College in New York City (1966-1988); participates in "Poets Against the Vietnam War Readings" organized by David Ray and Robert Bly. Meets Galway Kinnell and Edith Anne (Annie) Runk, school teacher.
1967- Marries Anne in New York City in April. Couple begins retreats at Lake Minnewaska outside of New Paltz, NY. Teaches summer session at Milwaukee. *Twenty Poems of Pablo Neruda.*
1968- Shall We Gather at the River (Wesleyan Univ. Press).
POEMS TREATING THIS ERA: "Having Lost My Sons, I Confront the Wreckage of the Moon: Christmas 1960," "Voices Between Waking and Sleeping in the Mountains," "Outside Fargo, North Dakota," "A Poem Written Under the Archway…," "Two Postures Beside a Fire," "Revelation," "Mary Bly," "Two Drunks," "Hook."

1970's

1970- A Rockefeller Foundation grant allows Wrights to travel to France, Italy, Austria, and to Yugoslavia; joined in Vienna by sons Franz and Marshall. *Poems of Herman Hesse* (Farrar, Straus & Giroux) translated by James Wright.
1971- Collected Poems (Wesleyan Univ. Press), wins Pulitzer Prize in 1972. Teaches in Montreal.
1973- Death of father, Dudley; begins writing in prose; *Two Citizens* (Farrar, Straus, & Giroux.)
1974- Death of mother, Jessie. Teaches summer session in Buffalo, NY; hospitalized for mental stress

Annie and James in San Gimigiana, Italy, photo by Jane Lee 1979.

and exhaustion. Wright receives honorary degree from Kenyon College.

1976- Travels to Honolulu to teach summer session at University of Hawaii, visits with John Logan and W. S. Merwin. *Moments of the Italian Summer* (Dryan Press.)

1977- Summer travels to France and Italy. *To a Blossoming Pear Tree* (Farrar, Straus, Giroux.)

1978- Guggenheim Award, travels in Europe; begins long correspondence with native American author Leslie Marmon Silko.

1979- Returns to U.S. in Sept. with a sore throat which leads to doctor visit and diagnosis of his throat cancer,

hospitalized in New York's Mount Sinai.

1980's & Beyond

1980- Attends White House tribute to American posted by Jimmy and Rosalynn Carter. Transferred to Calvary Hospital for terminal cancer patients, visited by many friends and family. Wright dies March 25 of cancer to the tongue.

First Annual James Wright Poetry Festival in his hometown of Martins Ferry, OH.

Poems treating this era: "Honey," "One Last Look at the Adige: Verona in the Rain," "Piccolini," "Two Moments in Rome," "Two Moments in Venice."

1981- *The Summers of James and Annie Wright* (Sheepmeadow Press*)*, *Leave It to the Sunlight* and *A Reply to Matthew Arnold* (chapbooks by Logbridge-Rhodes Press)

1982- *This Journey: Poems* (Random House)

1983- *The Collected Prose of James Wright* (Univ. of Michigan Press)

1985- *A Secret Field* (Logbridge-Rhodes)

1986- *The Shape of Light* (White Pine Press) *The Delicacy of Lace: Letters Between Leslie Marmon Silko and James Wright* (Graywolf Press)

1988- *James Wright's Ohio* (docu-drama video project by Tom Koba & Larry Smith, co-sponsored by Ohio Arts Council and Ohio Humanities Council).

1990- *Above the River: The Complete Poems*, with introduction by Donald Hall (Wesleyan University Press)

2003- Son Franz writes *Walking to Martha's Vineyard* (Alfred A. Knopf, 2003) which received a Pulitzer Prize.

James and Annie Wright, photo by John Untrecker, c. 1970's.

As I Walk on Whiskey Island in Winter, I Think of James Wright

Mary O'Malley

> *I began in Ohio,*
> *I still think of home*
> James Wright (1927 – 1980)

James, if you reach down hard enough with me
through the Cleveland dirt layers of shale and garbage earth
you and I might touch dreams

and failed seeds of Irish root mothers those without
names, frayed rope lives tied down on tin shanty roofs far
from the bright sun of Western Ireland's night.

We might find stained glass from St. Mary's of the Flats
bottles of holy water blessed by Amadeus Rappe
here on this island, on the edge of a sliding city
at the beginning of another century

of already too much pain. Your finger bones could rise
from the grave and help me scribe the sounds of broken
rosary beads buried in unsanctified

ground, candled hymns and High Mass lights, hidden
baptisms and rectory marriages, intertwined with blessings
from knotted Carmelite rope.

The cracked tea cup stained brown inside
at the bottom leaves of green tea gone
like the reader and her readings.

And further on to the south and west
past hills time and swamp tales of Ohio Cirty, we could discover
petrified tracks patiently waiting inside clay cliffs or fields
of abandoned story You could

help me find words, create heel and toe casts from Cleveland
Steel's hired Pinkerton men; or my grandfather and his union
friends hiding out at night-

afraid to go home and bring the weight of violent
shoes to narrow wooden steps. We two, could shine
halogen lights and search

for the trace and smell of sweat hanging from haloed images
of longshoremen's heads; the boyos fresh from the docks,
as they stood at the main corner of the Angle,

Detroit and old Pearl; watching greenhorn girls
walk past after a day of service with the millionaires on Euclid Avenue;
Unaware of the future

only we can see; a cathedral wedding and twelve
priest Mass, or lives magnetized by bar stools
and beer bottles.

All mere memory shapes; holograms and dance shoes
sticking to us like nightclothes on hot summer nights.
But maybe, all we can find

are residue of oak tree limbs fallen and scattered
into an American hope for coal blooming into diamonds of rust
while the Midwest lake and its ceaseless winds
embrace a crying banshee reconnoitering for the soul ashes
of the forgotten dead.

JAMES WRIGHT, THE PERSON BEHIND THE POEMS

A Wild Perfection: The Selected Letters of James Wright,
eds. Anne Wright and Saundra Rose Maley, with Jonathan Blunk.
NY: Farrar, Straus, Giroux 2005, 633 pgs.
A REVIEW BY LARRY SMITH

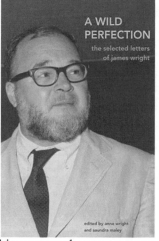

Something comes over me when I read a book I really love and feel the significance of—a deep connection and urge to share it with others. Maybe it's the teacher in me, maybe it's the need to talk about it with friends, maybe it's the call of the reviewer, but I think it's something all book lovers must feel. In the case of Ohio poet James Wright's *Selected Letters*, I thought of a hundred fellow-poets whose work has been informed by Wright's. So, it may not be for everyone, but if you're a contemporary poet or an avid reader of such writing, it's a revealing and insightful book for you.

Not only was Wright a fine, skilled poet in the 1950s, adept at traditional iambics and a smoothness of style, he is revealed here as one who struggled to give birth to a new verse and himself as a 'sincerist' poet, one who moves from the love of form into a more dangerous and engaged career as poet of the authentic. In the vortex of the late 1950s he joined a host of poets breaking from traditional formalism into the bold and open field of free verse: Louis Simpson, W. D. Snodgrass, Denise Levertov, Galway Kinnell, Richard Hugo, Stanley Kunitz, and others, in particular friends James Dickey and Robert Bly, all of whom he corresponded with.

The breakthrough letters to Dickey and Bly from 1958-1960 are worth the price of the book (or the trip to the library). Here we witness how the birth of this "new imagination" writing also included the death of the old training and models for these poets By this time Wright had made it through high school at Martins Ferry, done a tour in the Army in Japan, graduated from Kenyon College, married high school sweetheart Liberty Kovacs, had a son Franz (the poet) while studying in Vienna, done graduate work at University of Washington in Seattle, and moved to what he considered desolate Minneapolis, Minnesota. Surprisingly he is also pretty hard on his Ohio homeland in the letters, revealing his love-hate relationship with "that place" about which he could not stop writing.

Nothing really new here, except that these letters reveal the depth of Wright's personal struggle with his identity as poet. Even after winning the Yale Younger Poets Prize and the publication of his *The Green Wall* collection (a book he considered "dead" by 1958), Wright doubts himself deeply. "So I quit," he writes to Donald Hall. "I have been betraying whatever was true and courageous (how nothing's that!) in myself and in everyone else for so long, that I am still fairly convinced that I have killed it. So I quit." It's an oath he will relent of a month later, one brought on by a stinging review of contemporary poets by James Dickey in *Sewanee Review*. At first

Wright sends a flaming letter to Dickey accusing him of assassinating some fine fellow poets (himself included), then in a second six page letter apologetically relents and admits the truth of Dickey's accusation that formalism has sucked the life out of contemporary verse, his own work worst among them. This lively correspondence is included as well as his earliest concurrent writings to Robert Bly, making life-long friends with both men.

We witness from inside the poet's mind and heart the triple passions of his life—family, literature, and poetry. He proclaims loudly his attachment to poets of the new imagination, including Walt Whitman, Rene Char, George Trakl, Pablo Neruda, and Federico Garcia Lorca, considering Lorca's *The Poet in New York* and his "Ode to Walt Whitman" the model for the new verse he would write. In the correspondence this dramatic transformation comes alive as we are brought close to his motives, intentions, and to the personalities of these pioneering poets of the new. We watch Wright struggle with personal relationships, an emotional instability compounded by alcoholism, an ambivalent identity with place and poetry. Here is the person behind the poems, the poet driven to a "wild perfection" (a Kunitz line). Peter Stitts' promised biography is now decades overdue, and so this book fills a huge gap. Included are letters to family, friends, and a huge cast of poets from Theodore Roethke to Leslie Marmon Silko.

As though this were not enough, editors Annie Wright (James' second wife) and Saundra Maley provide a basic chronology, scant chapter introductions that include fine period photos of the poet, and a 46 page appendix of Wright's early and unpublished poems, along with biographical sketches of correspondents and an index. Wright's lovely poem to his young wife, Libby, "To a Girl Heavy with Child" though never collected, is one he himself considered among his finest:

> …what is my human share
> In seeing your body, as my body, slacken,
> Shudder and pray beneath the burning air
> Till the long dawn rinses your skin like rain?
> Love is the child I bear, and love is pain.

All poetry lovers owe a debt of gratitude for the compilers of this book.

RESONATING NEWNESS

Wood smoke & Green Tea, By Russell Salamon
2006; 66pp; Deep Cleveland Press
P.O. Box 14248, Cleveland, OH 44114.
A REVIEW BY MICHAEL McMAHON

Russell Salamon—one of the original visionaries of the mimeo revolution of the sixties, friend of d. a. levy, and author of *Descent into Cleveland*—reminds us once again of the significance of art and the radical states of awareness that poetry engenders. In this new book of poems you get the definite sense of the sacred in nature, but more important: the nature of what is sacred. All things are wound in the eternal word (something posted in existence)—the poetry; life itself; the infinite now; the beautiful.

These poems are spacious enough for fractals of infinite discovery and yet simple enough to display the universe in a starfish. In his poem "Blue Like a Memory" words float in and out of the human condition and into timelessness: "The sea carries all colors, mostly blue./ Blue like a memory of fingers touching/ for the first time in deep daylight/ when we were open and had forgotten/ the centuries. Its silver mirrors paint/ high mountains and forests, and if you/ forget the stars you can see them/ swimming among starfish." An overwhelming rush is accomplished at the crescendo of every completed thought by brilliant twists of juxtaposed images and ideas. Creation, mind, self, individual objects in nature…all touch a common foundation and are effortlessly expressed from existence without differentiation. Salamon's distinct voice burns with an abstract aesthetic capable of wording the un-wordable—synthesizing the matter into molten expressions.

As fluid and elemental as this work is, it never loses the human perspective. The intensity of souls wrapped in the ecstatic-romantic is central throughout. In the poem "Woodsmoke and Green Tea" the erotic is elevated to its rightful place in the purity of everlasting love: "He kissed her where her dreams/ fainted from exhaustion. He was/ water in her roses; she was musk/ on his fingertips.// Before dawn they had already lived/ the length of a long river." In many places the wedding theme is evoked with as much elegance, pomp, and passion as a Palestrina Motet. In "Wedding Poem" the imagery of paradise enhances the lightness and resonating newness of total union: "The pink long stemmed/ girls of honor/ slip out of/ the distance/ down the stairs/ to the music of gods and angels// while the bride/ already smiling from eternal/ joys walks with paradise/ in her feet/ to join/ the time stream of/ his arms."

Sexual longing becomes indiscernible from spiritual desire to rejoin with creation. In "Red Dress" physical sensation is taken over by metaphysical release: "When I see you in your red dress/ I want to become darkness so that/ you are a flame as you walk by/ and I whisper evening birds/ into your hair//. . .You set into my eyes like music/ and all the colors speak luscious/ sentences. How green the world is/ now that you have said it." Salamon illuminates the imperfect symmetry of natural order that balances all of creation from the self-guiding, co-creating viewpoint of love. His poetry speaks simplicity and yet the mystery he awakens (through startling color and jolting affirmation) is left sacred—incomprehensible to reason.

The graphically beautiful motion and pulse of the poems is offset by the poignantly direct ejaculations that shift gears to an almost Patchen-like reverence and enlightened awe. In "Impossible Beauty" the poem reads like the whisper of a secret prayer, a posited light of concealed optimism for the human race:

> We are impossibly beautiful
> so we make ourselves possible
> by being scarab beetles or frogs
> or sedge plants. You take up
> a perfect girl shape and swing
> its arms and hips until the sky falls. . .
>
> The world/ knows us in our infinite beauty,
> but won't tell.. . .
>
> But our faces are never seen,
> they are too beautiful. I feel you
> with my beauty, and out nets of lives
> and loves cast solid shadows that stand
> as buildings and voices in night air.. . .
>
> Time is a lie told/ to hide our free faces until we
>   see
> with deep spaces who touches us.

Salamon's repudiation of all that hinders or holds back life is exacted in resignation, but never defeat. The energy of each poem beckons toward renewal, and creates (as true art always should) clear streams of rejuvenating possibilities. This is a book to be treasured because with all its complex intention and energy it still delights with softness of wind, and leaf and wave; and urges hope through quiet reflection and magical wisps of extraordinary insight. Trust me, you'll want to read it cover to cover.

THE HEARTLANDS CREDITS...2006

Alan S. Ambrisco (Akron, OH) was born in western New York and moved to the Midwest to work on his PhD at Indiana University. He is currently an associate professor of English and assistant chair for the English Department at The University of Akron, and specializes in Chaucer and Middle English literature.

Kaye Bache-Snyder (Longmont, CO) grew up in Toledo, graduated from Ohio State University. She publishes short stories, nonfiction, photographs, features, reviews, and poetry and teaches at the Arvada Center for the Arts and Humanities.

Lois Barliant (Chicago, IL) grew up in Colorado. Her BA is from St. Olaf and her MA in English from the University of Chicago. A member of several writing workshops, she is also an editor at the *Chicago Quarterly Review*.

Boyd Bauman (Kansas City, MO) is originally from outside Bern, Kansas (population 200). He currently teaches and writes in the Kansas City area. "Hatchet Job" is dedicated to the people of the south wind now living under neon casino signs.

Emily Bobo (KS) has performed her work nationally in New York, Colorado, Nebraska, Kansas, and New Mexico. She holds an MFA from Wichita State University and is currently completing a doctorate in English at the University of Kansas.

Gary Buslik (Chicago, IL) teaches creative writing at the University of Illinois. His essays and short stories appear in many commercial and literary magazines. The selection here is from his book-in-progress, *A Rotten Person Travels the West Indies*.

William DeGenaro (MI) teaches creative writing, working-class studies, and composition at the University of Michigan Dearborn. He conducts research centering on working-class education and culture and is editor of the forthcoming *Who Says? Working-Class Rhetoric, Class Consciousness, and Community* (University of Pittsburgh Press.)

Judith Ford is a psychotherapist and writer whose fiction and poetry have appeared in many literary journals. She has been nominated twice for Pushcart prizes, for poetry in 2000 and for fiction in 2001. She won the 2005 Willow Review Award for Prose. She is currently working on a memoir, *Fever of Unknown Origin.*

Paul Freidinger (IL) was born and grew up in central Illinois farm country. For the last 33 years he has taught English in Frankfort, Illinois. He has a creative nonfiction piece due this fall in *Gulf Stream.* A new venture will include reviewing novels for the *San Diego Union-Tribune.*

Sammy Greenspan (Cleveland Heights, OH) has a poem forthcoming in *Del Sol Review*. She is a member of the Pudding House Salon poetry workshop.

Andrew W. Grossman was born in Ecuador in 1943 and was raised in Cleveland Heights, OH, after emigrating at age 2. He is married and has one son and two daughters. For 35 years he worked as a technical writer and has published a technical book on telecommunications systems (1984), and numerous news articles in local papers.

Mike Hampton (Cincinnati, OH) is a graduate of Spalding University's MFA in Writing Program. He has recently finished his first novel, and is in the process of completing a short story collection which includes the story featured here.

Carol Hattrup (Kansas City, MO) lives with her woodworking husband, a son, and three dogs in a forty year old house which she and her husband are renovating. She recently taught second grade, and, prior to that, was a technical writer at a Fortune 100 company.

Joanne Jacobson grew up in the Chicago suburb of Evanston, and has lived in Iowa, France's Loire Valley, Vermont and New York City. She is a professor of English and associate dean for academic affairs at Yeshiva College, where she teaches American literature, American studies and creative writing. Her memoir, *Hunger Artist,* is due out in Fall 2007 from Bottom Dog Press.

Walter Knupfer (MI) was born in Evanston, Illinois. He was educated at The University of Iowa where he received a BA, MFA from the Writers' Workshop, an MA and PhD. Now disabled, he works as a volunteer, assisting Aphasia patients at the University of Michigan's University Center for the Development of Language and Literacy.

Steve Koelsch (Sandusky, OH.) He grew up in Ohio, graduated from Bowling Green State University with a BA in psychology, then an MBA from California National University. He is recently retired from a global pharmaceutical company, writes poetry and fiction, and enjoys sculpting and clay mono-printing. He received a Vermont Studio Center Fellowship in Poetry 2006.

Jane K. Kretschmann (Piqua, OH) is a native of Alabama and she teaches at a community college. Recently some of her poems were broadcast on *Theme and Variations,* an NPR program, and *Art Waves,* on WKRC in New York City.

Dale M. Kushner studied at the C.G. Jung Institute in Switzerland and teaches workshops on dreams, fairy tales, and writing. Her current manuscript, *Via Magdalene*, was a finalist for the Agah Shahid Ali Prize in Poetry, The Tupelo Press Award, The Prairie Schooner Award and the Tom Wick Prize in Poetry as well as a Wisconsin Arts Board Grant in the Literary Arts. She is finishing a novel.

Rebecca Lilly (Charlottesville, VA) has one book on spiritual philosophy and practice, "The Insights of Higher

Awareness" (Humanics), and two collections of poetry, "You Want to Sell Me a Small Antique (Gibbs Smith), and "Shadwell Hills" (Birch Brook Press.)

Michael McMahon (Huron, OH) is an associate editor at Bottom Dog Press, a student at Firelands College BGSU, and the author of a series of chapbooks, including his recent *Golden Tongue Tree* (Hypnogog Press 2006.)

Ken Meisel (Detroit, MI) is a poet & psychotherapist. He is the author of two chapbooks entitled *Before Exit* (March Street Press.) He writes that "poetry, the act of writing it, is one of the habits I engage in that assists me toward accepting reality the way it is, as it is."

Mitchell Metz a former All-Ivy football player, he is now the primary caregiver for his four young children. He is currently a Pushcart nominee.

Wendy Jones Nakanishi (Japan) grew up in a small town in northern Indiana, and then went to Britain, where she earned an MA and a PhD in eighteenth-century English literature at the universities of Lancaster and Edinburgh. She has resided in Japan for over twenty years, and is a member of staff at a small private Japanese university.

Mary O'Malley has an MFA from Spalding Univerity in Louisville, Kentucky and has been a social worker for over twenty years. She is also a mother of two sets of twins.

Anne Panning (NY) has published a book of short stories, *The Price of Eggs* (Coffeehouse Press), as well as short fiction and nonfiction. Anne has completed a novel, *Good News Girls!* (winner *Cecil B. Hackney Award* for novels), as well as another collection of stories, *Super America*. She lives with her husband and two children, and teaches creative writing at SUNY-Brockport.

Laura Elizabeth Pearson (Berlin Hts., OH) is named for two grandmother-storytellers and is soon to be a grandmother herself. She is fine actress and tireless in her efforts for peace and harmony through her work as teacher, performer, massage therapist and shaman.

Mark Putzi received his MA in creative writing in December of 1989. Prior to 1990, he published two short stories.but he never wrote poetry until the mid '90's.

Doug Ramspeck (Lima, OH) directs the Writing Center and teaches creative writing and composition at the Ohio State University at Lima. He lives with his wife, Beth, and their sixteen-year-old daughter, Lee.

Sara Jane Rattan (Milwaukee, WI) lives with her husband and two sons, and she writes fiction, essays and poetry. She holds a BA from Lawrence University and a JD from Marquette University Law School, but says that her real education has taken place in the writing workshops at Redbird Studios. "IKEA & Me" is her second published story.

Bruce Selyem (Bozeman, Montana)is a professional photographer and founded the Country Grain Elevator Historical Society to collect, preserve and share the elevator's legacy. His photos are in the book *The Art of Country Grain Elevators* (Bottom Dog Press, 2005). He did the cover art for this issue of *Heartlands.*

Knute Skinner (County Clare, Ireland) retired from his position at Western Washington University. His most recent full-length collection is "Stretches" (Salmon Publishing.) His collection "The Other Shoe" won the 2004-2005 Pavement Saw Chapbook Award.

Carol Smallwood's work has appeared in *English Journal*, *Poesia*, *Lady Churchill's Rosebud Wristlet*, *Poesia*, *Iris*, and several others. *Educators as Writers: Writing for Personal and Professional Development* is forthcoming from Peter Lang. She didn't have the courage to begin poetry until recently.

Larry Smith (Huron, OH) is a professor emeritus of BGSU Firelands College and the director of Bottom Dog Press. His eighth book of poetry is *A River Remains: Poems* (WordTech Editions, 2006.) He was born and raised in Mingo Junction, Ohio, 20 miles north of James Wright's Martins Ferry. Wright was his initial inspiration to be a poet. The *James Wright's Ohio* video program by Smith and Tom Koba is available through Bottom Dog Press.

Rodney Torreson was born in 1951 and grew up on a farm in northwest Iowa. For many years he has taught in a Lutheran parochial school in Grand Rapids, MI. He is the author of a chapbook, *On a Moonstruck Gravel Road* (Juniper Press, 1994) and two full-length collections, *The Ripening of Pinstripes: Called Shots on the New York Yankees* (Story Line Press, 1998) and *A Breathable Light* (New Issues Press, 2002).

Troy Tradup (Minneapolis, MN) is currently writing a werewolf novel to counteract all of the classic literature he's subjected himself to recently. His stage adaptation of Charles Dickens's *Hard Times* opens in the Twin Cities this fall. His stage adaptation of *The Island of Dr. Moreau* was recently published by Playscripts, Inc.

Jon Volkmer directs the creative writing program at Ursinus College. He received his Ph.D. in English from the University of Nebraska, his MA in Creative Writing from the University of Denver. His recent book is *The Art of Country Grain Elevators: Poems by Jon Volkmer and Photographs by Bruce Selyem* (Bottom Dog Press 2005.)

Michael E. Waldecki (Lorain, OH) is a veteran of the Vietnam and the poetry wars. His many chapbooks and two collections of verse are available through Bottom Dog Press.

David Michael Wolach is 28 years old and grew up just outside of Detroit. He received degrees in neuroscience (from Sarah Lawrence College) and philosophy (Columbia University), then became a union organizer in New York. As of late he has dedicated himself to writing almost full-time. He is currently finishing a first novel, *Panopticon.*"

Marce Wood (MN) lives in a humble home on the jaggedy shores of Lake Superior. She is an artist, a counselor and a poet who embraces a life full of loving family, laughing friends, glowing children and furry companions.

CALL FOR SUBMISSIONS:

HEARTLANDS: A MAGAZINE OF MIDWEST LIFE & ART
VOLUME FIVE

Our intended audience begins with the Firelands Area and extends to Northwest Ohio, Ohio at large, the Midwest, and the nation. We are looking for ideas, photo stories, interviews, clusters of poems-fiction-essays around our theme of *Midwest Life and Art*.

➡ **NONFICTION:** Query the editor with articles on the theme of Midwest Art and Writing, 500 - 4000 words. [Nancy Dunham ndcat@adelphia.net]

➡ **POETRY:** Send 3-5 poems on the theme [Editors: David Shevin & Lin Ryan-Thompson]

➡ **FICTION:** Send 1-2 stories on the theme. 4,500 words maximum. [Editor: Connie Willett Everett]

➡ **ART:** We are seeking photography primarily, but some nature drawings may be accepted. [Query the editor: Becky Dickerson, becky@finegrainphotography.com]

➡ **OUR READERS WRITE:** Email submissions on question to be established. Query the editor, Susanna Sharp-Schwacke, sgail1@sbcglobal.net.

➡ **PAYMENT:** $10-$20 plus 2 copies

➡ **MANAGING EDITOR:** Larry Smith [Lsmithdog@aol.com]

Deadline for the issue is May 15, 2007
Please submit poems, essays, fiction & art between January 1, 2007 and May 15, 2007.
Please send manuscripts with a Self-Addressed Stamped Envelope to:
HEARTLANDS
Firelands Writing Center
BGSU Firelands/ One University Dr.
Huron, Ohio 44839

The Firelands Writing Center supports the art of writing and art in the Great Lakes Region.
It is supported in part by grants from the Ohio Arts Council and is distributed through Small Press Distribution:
http://www.theheartlandstoday.net/

For a copy of any of our issues, please submit requests to:
Firelands Writing Center
BGSU Firelands/ One University Dr.
Huron, Ohio 44839

© Bruce Selyem, 2006